Ebee Wo

We Made It!

On The Farm
During The Depression

By
Elree B. Worley

We Made It!
Published by Yawn's Publishing
210 East Main Street
Canton, GA 30114
www.yawnsbooks.com

This book was previously printed in two volumes as "Rounding The Corners" and "We Made It!"

ISBN13: 978-0-9818673-7-3
ISBN10: 0-9818673-7-5

Printed in the United States

Dedication

This book is lovingly dedicated to my dear granddaughter, Dyanna, who wanted to hear all about what I did as a child; to my daughter, Penelope, who encouraged me to put the little stories in a book; and to my husband, Clyde, who was forced to listen to each and every story; to my generous and exceptional daughter, Deborah and son Daniel, along with my precious little grandson, Christopher.

With my sincerest thanks to all of my sisters and brothers and parents who helped create all of these situations, and solved a lot of the problems in order to "Make It" through those trying times.

Introduction

These stories are indeed authentic as far as they go. They were written partially for enjoyment and partially to preserve the family activities and traditions of that era and locale. They are intended to acquaint readers from another time frame with the everyday life and special occasions of a typical large family just prior to, during and immediately following the big depression.

The hub of this community was located at a crossroads and was composed of two general merchandise stores with gas pumps, a barber shop, a cotton gin, a corn mill, a garage (complete with one weekend mechanic), a nearby schoolhouse and a church. With hardly any exceptions all of the houses were family owned and a great number of the families were related. Each was a good neighbor and very conservative in their views.

Because of the very modern "eavesdropper" telephone service, everyone stayed informed about all the community happenings. There were no secrets.

When the chores were taken care of, the men congregated at the general stores and exchanged news and hearsays about the surrounding "mini-boroughs" which were a few miles away.

During these years of hardships, time was at a standstill, there were no noticeable changes nor progress. All names of persons and places have intentionally been withheld.

It is hoped that these stories will bring back old memories and lend enjoyment and enlightenment to the reader.

Some people refer to these years as the "Good Ole Days", but all things considered, it doesn't sound like the most appropriate choice of words.

Contents

Meals And Their Preparation   1
The Sure Cures   4
Transportation In The Country   6
Doctor – Doctor   9
Fun And Games – Homespun Of Course   12
Cleaning The House And Yard   16
Spring Planting   19
Going To Meetin   21
Saturday P.M. Visitation   24
New Dresses For The Girls   26
Saturday Grooming   29
Catching The School Bus   31
School Daze   34
Whether To Stay Home Or Go   38
Reading Material   40
Chicken Raising   43
Slopping The Hogs   45
Seven Maids A Milking   47
In Search Of A Turkey Nest   50
The Call Of The Wild
         (Ripe Blackberries)   52
The Bedbug Era   55
The Family Reunion   57
When It Snowed   60
Sunday Evenin' Singings   63
The Shaving Ritual   66
Getting Ready For Christmas   68
When The Radio Got Turned On   71
The Square Dances   75
Beloved Tacky Parties   77
The Box Suppers   79
A Hunting We Did Go   81
Candy Pulling   83
The Wash Hole   85
The Big Deep Gully   87

The Monumental Family Tree 90
The Delicacy Of Delicacies:
      "Homemade Ice Cream" 92
Saga Of The Mad Dog 94
Saving The Chewing Gum 97
Watermelon Cutting 99
The Dual Purpose Scuppernong Vines 102
The Fruit Drying Process 104
The Original One-Size-Fits-All 106
By-words:
      Slang Or Personal Expressions 108
We Had A Tobacco Chewer 111
Beloved Paths 113
The Medicine Shows 116
When Court Was In Session 119
Homework Or A Reasonable Facsimile 123
Cooking On The 'Wood Stove' 126
A Tribute To Granny 129
Discipline According To The Bible 132
'Looking After' Each Other 135
Welcomed Hand-Me-Downs 138
Necessary Mending 141
Making Soap From Scratch 144
Wash Day 146
Exciting Rolling Stores 149
Making Syrup   For Better Or Worse 152
Road Scrape Spectacle 155
Churning 158
Easter In The Country 161
Building Them Barbed Wire Fences 164
Making A Vegetable Garden 167
Summer Storms 171
Readying A Barbecue 174
The Community Blacksmith 177
Sharpening Up The Tools By Hand 180
When Bees Swarmed 183
Cotton Pickin' Time 186
Picnics In The Wilds 189
Fish Fries In The Rough 192

August Meeting 'A Country   195
Bugs And Games With Them   199
Hog Killing Episodes   202
Corn Shuckings   206
Plotting The Preserves   210
Spending The Night With Granny   214
Gathering Mule Feed (Fodder)   218
Revolutionary Basket Weaving   221
Checkers And Set Back Experts   224
Learning The "Two-Step"   227
Scarecrow   229
A Squirrel Hunt   232
Setting A Rabbit Box ("Gums")   235
Hiding The Booze Bottles   237
Quilting Techniques   240
Doomed Birds Of A Feather   243
The Art Of Whittling   247
Star Gazing   250
Exciting Cake Walks   253
Good Ole Country Music   257
When Santa Finally Came   260
When Anyone Died In
       "Our Neck Of The Woods"   263
Restlessness Amid Poverty   266
Along Came Relief   270

Meals And Their Preparation

Our poor ole mother was always cooking and cleaning and planning for the next meal. We simply did not eat out. There weren't many cafes, none close by, plus you didn't have money to spare, nor the transportation. A crowd like ours almost never got invited out, except on rare occasions to some relative's house.

Most of the time, we all ate like horses and were always hungry. We didn't keep little snacks sitting around, so when mealtime came we were eager and waiting.

Sometime in the winter between meals, we'd find a cold biscuit, turn it sideways, bore a hole in it with our fingers and fill it up with sorghum syrup. This was very good except the syrup was bad to run down on your arms and clothes. We could get a raw potato from the dirt bank, or in the summer, if fruit was on the trees or berries on the bush (green or otherwise), we'd munch on those.

In the mornings, as soon as our dad had made a fire in the kitchen stove, our mom would hurry in and get the biscuits started. She'd mash together a big wade of dough (made with fresh lard, home-ground flour, a big pinch of baking soda, and buttermilk) in the huge bread tray and pinch off and pat up between 35 and 50 biscuits the first thing; then she'd scramble up all the eggs we had while the "sack sausage" or fat-back fried and the Louisiana Coffee boiled. Each morning, we'd have to open up a fresh pint of jam or jelly which was always homemade.

During the fall we'd just have sorghum syrup. The proper way to eat that was to smash up butter in a large blob of syrup, get a hot buttered biscuit, and "sop" it up. This often went on for minutes 'cause you had to make the syrup mixture and bread come out even.

Just as soon as breakfast was over and all those dirty dishes were washed and dried and put up, someone was making plans for dinner (lunch in some circles).

Incidentally, all of our dishwater was kept in a container for the hogs. This we called "slop". It also contained all the scraps that the dogs wouldn't eat. This same procedure followed each and every meal.

Most of the time, when we were through washing and drying dishes from one meal, we'd set the table for the next. We'd wipe off the "oil cloth" table cover; place the knives, forks, and spoons all around the table, putting the plates over them upside down to keep the flies and cats off. We'd round up jelly glasses of any description for the beverages and turn them upside down and have them ready also.

Lunches or dinners varied a lot 'cause we ate whatever we had on hand, canned or in the garden, and a lot of the time soups could be stretched to match the crowd, going on the assumption that a little more water or milk never hurt anyone. There was always an abundance of sweetened ice tea, except in cold weather.

If our mom could scratch up two or three vegetables and a meat or meat pie of a sort that would suffice, supplemented with pickles or cornbread and dessert or a "little something sweet," as my dad would say.

Those desserts were really varied. If she didn't have what the recipe called for, she'd substitute or even make up a dessert. Our super good one was made from biscuit dough, sugar, vanilla, and butter – to resemble little pinwheels and covered with water. When sufficiently browned, these were scrumptious but oh so fattening! It was good that we didn't know anything about calories. Back then, if a youngster was overweight, we just thought she'd taken after "Aunt Mollie" or her mother (what they ate had nothing to do with it).

When we ran out of flour we had ground from home grown wheat, we had to resort to store bought flour. Those large 50 lb bags didn't last very long because bread was truly our staff of life. Those bags were decorated, coarsely woven, cotton ones that our mother guarded carefully for dish-drying cloths.

Our shortening was strictly home grown hog lard stored in large metal containers, along with fresh churned butter. This was used sparingly in order to have enough for the breakfast biscuits.

Supper (or dinner) was not our main meal. If there was one, it was probably dinner (lunch). Usually after that meal we would work till night and we needed that nourishment. At night we'd have leftovers, if there were any, a few easy to cook vegetables, or buttermilk and cornbread; in cold weather "hoe cakes" with syrup was a favorite with us kids.

One of the things that smelled the best and lasted the longest was home-made hominy. This was dried field corn shelled and cooked in ashes in a large black pot till it could be husked, then it was washed good and clean and cooked till the corn was tender. Small amounts were taken out, seasoned, and cooked. Sometimes a pot full would last a whole week.

In the fall, when we'd sold our cotton and had some money, we'd watch our Dad walking down the hill from the store with a big bag. We happily awaited his arrival to see what he had for supper. It was either two big cans of QQ Salmon, or several cans of oysters with soda crackers, for oyster soup, or maybe a chunk of cheese. Whatever it was, we considered it to be a real treat.

When company was coming, we'd put the big pot in the little one. Our mother would cook everything she knew how to fix. We'd have at least three meats, chicken pie, and Brunswick stew along with all kinds of vegetables, casseroles, pickles, relishes, salads, and at least three kinds of desserts. That sounded extravagant, but there were plenty of kids to eat all of the leftovers.

The best part of all that planning and entertaining was that the company always reciprocated in a short time and we were the lucky ones who had "picking choice" and got waited on.

3

The Sure Cures

If getting sick and missing school was fun to anyone else, it sure wasn't to us! We pretended to feel good when we really didn't - anything to escape the dreaded treatments! We'd stifle a sneeze, choke a cough, and sneak and wipe our noses on our sleeves trying to keep anyone from noticing our approaching illnesses.

Back then, there were three known and widely used medicines in our family circle and community. The number 1 remedy on everyone's cabinet shelf was castor oil. You drank it under a threat from your dad (the supreme punisher) with one hand holding your nose and the other ready to hold over your mouth to keep from vomiting. We were almost always given something real sweet or sour immediately afterward to kill the taste. Just tasting or swallowing it was bad enough, but the worst was yet to come. The tummy would growl, hurt and then the trips to the outside toilet would start – with the discovery of toilet tissue unknown in this area, your bottom sure got sore from using the newspaper or Sears Roebuck catalog. When the BM's went on into the night you had to use the "slop jar" and set it out on the porch till morning, at which time it was your duty to carry it away from the house, empty it, rinse it and return it to its rightful place under the bed.

Number 2 on the treatment list was "Epsom Salts". This harsh medicine was mostly used when you didn't have castor oil. It didn't matter where you hurt nor what the symptoms were, you were given the same medicine for everything. If one of them didn't help, it was assumed the other one would. Now this Epsom Salts was a real disaster. You sure needed a change of underwear when you took that stuff, 'cause it didn't fool around about kicking in. If this didn't help you very much and if you were strong enough you took the third wonder drug, "Calomel".

I'm sure this stuff was discovered by accident and would today be outlawed by the FDA, or recommended for some big, strong animal. This stuff was *strong!* If it had

4

been dosed out according to weight and age, you would have been given only 1/16 of one tablet; but, since the doctor had nothing to do with it, your parents just used their own judgment for a quick cure. You definitely had to go to bed when you took that crap. The only good thing about being that sick was you got boiled custard, milk toast, orange juice, and/or vanilla milk to help bring you back to life.

In cool weather, when colds, flu, pneumonia and other forms of distemper set in, the all sufficient bags of asphedity became the "smell of the day". The reason for this was such an effective deterrent was the fact that no one could get close enough to give you their germs.

When spring came we'd often get boils or little scratches that wouldn't heal up on schedule, so we were forced to take several doses of sulphur and molasses. This mixture was thought to purify your blood. After or during these dosages, our dad would apply tallow (a homemade grease made from cattle fat), or camphor, or Watkins ointment to the affected area, and sure enough, in a week or two it would heal up.

The little illnesses like measles, chicken-pox, and whooping cough were to be expected, and they just ran their course – no big deal. If you ran a high fever you got to go to bed and get some extra "waiting on", but if you sang too loud, or it looked like you were having any fun you had to vacate the bed and go on back to school or join the labor forces in the fields.

Transportation In The Country

In our community distant visiting and shopping was kept to a minimum, and transportation was the reason why. If you had a car, you needed tires, and then you had to borrow a tag. In the winter time it was too cold in the old Model A's or T's (ford), and in the summer time it was too hot and always too crowded in the car.

The old unpaved country roads fit into three categories; bad, impossible, and worse. In the first place, they must have been laid out by someone following a snake. It was almost impossible to pass another vehicle or even an animal, plus the fact that they had ruts or washed out holes so deep they'd jar your innards trying to get over them. If springs or shocks for cars had been invented, you couldn't tell it from riding in our car.

In the summer the dust was so bad you could hardly breathe, and when you arrived your freshly starched and ironed clothes looked like you'd been playing in a pig pen. If you rolled the windows up you'd almost suffocate and sweat so profusely you didn't look any better.

Often the driver, who was always an older man, would stop in the middle of the road 15 to 20 times to see how the neighbor's corn and cotton looked or to speak to someone on the side of the road, who'd be walking along real slow with his hands fastened behind his back and a big wad of chewing tobacco in his month. Back then everybody had time to talk. Occasionally we'd see someone digging a storm pit, which served a dual purpose; mostly they were used to store flowers in the winter.

We were really lucky when we didn't have a "blow out" either going or coming. One of the best parts of the trip was getting to blow the horn at a pig, dog or chickens in the road. When you pressed down on that horn and heard that "ahhhhhooooga" everybody came running out in the yard to see what it was. Everyone's car horn sounded a little bit different, so we knew who was blowing their horn at any given time.

One of the most dreaded things we had to encounter was getting "stuck" in rainy or wet weather. When you got bogged down in that red mud there was no easy way out and certainly no wrecker service. Only the passengers could free the wheels after much shoving and pushing; piling rocks and limbs in the ruts was usually the only way we could begin to get the ole "flivver" going. We'd be so splattered with mud when we got the car unstuck we'd hardly recognize each other. Our shoes had to be scraped and wiped with a stick or rock or weeds so we could get back in the car.

I don't remember ever running out of gas. The car was kicked out of gear running down the hills to save gas or maybe the car could run on fumes? Most of the time it was loaded to capacity and sometimes a few folks were hanging on the running boards.

Whenever we'd cross over a rickety old wooden creek or river bridge, we'd all try to sit light so as not to cave the bridge in. A lot of little streams had no bridge, so we'd ford them, get a little splashed and cooled off. Then we'd proceed at our usual 10-15 miles an hour – plenty of time to get to wherever we were going.

All of the windows seldom worked at one time, so we usually took along an extra wrap to divert the wind or rain. The airiness of the car was also a blessing. With that many people inside there was bound to be some odor involved, but it couldn't linger very long. The door handles were just as unpredictable but presented no real problems. We just climbed over the front seats to the nearest available exit, and the boys would climb out the windows if they were in a big hurry.

Stopping for the rest rooms was quite different back then – there were none – even at home. The car was stopped and the unfortunate one who had to "go" scrambled out, found a good deep ditch out of sight or hid behind the nearest bush, and soon we'd all be on our way again.

The only other things that detained us when we were on one of those trips were a snake in the road or some almost ripe plums on the side of the road. The snake had to be killed one way or another, and there was no way we were gonna pass up those plums!

Doctor - Doctor

We never knew doctors were interested in our well-being. We just thought they were all "booger men" who liked to torture people.

The only doctors we ever saw were old men (or looked old) with fat stomachs and glasses - they weren't friendly. I don't ever remember seeing one of them smile; sometimes they'd even make us take off some of our clothes, which was most embarrassing.

Their offices were dull, often dark rooms with sad looking colors and not even enough chairs if there were very many of us.

In the first place, we had to be critically ill to even be considered a candidate for a doctor's visit, whether at our house or his office. When I was very young, I thought their only mission in life was to bring new babies to our house, and we already had a house full of kids! In fact, on one occasion, one of my younger sisters told the doctor he ought to be taking them back instead of bringing them in. For this reason alone, there was ample reason to dislike them.

When and if we were forced to go to the doctor, our parents would line up some transportation, give us a bath, and round up some whole underwear. Sometimes we had to borrow slips or panties from another kid so as to be presentable and make a good impression. All of this taken care of, we'd get underway, accompanied by our mother.

We were frightened to death and too timid to even tell the doctor our names, our mother would always prompt us with, "Betty Lou, tell the doctor your name." After several questions he'd look in our ears, which we were sure he was going to amputate, check out our eyes, ask us if we could read three-inch letters across the room, look in our mouth and mash our tongue down with a small "plank" till we gagged, and then ask us to say "Ahhhh, real big." To which we'd reply, "Ahhhh Big." He

9

thought it was funny, but we didn't see the humor. We were sitting there all tensed up, waiting for that dread diagnosis, "We'd better give her a shot," - but much to our "liking," he'd just prescribe some of that old familiar calomel or Epsom salts, or castor oil, along with a special diet and sometimes he'd suggest a teaspoon of cod liver oil per day - *that was real good news!?*

We nearly always got some bed rest out of the deal. I loved to "draw and paint," so that was worth all the other harassment, plus all the other kids were a lot nicer to you when you were sick.

On one occasion I had gotten a shot for some reason or other, and when I got through describing the horrible ordeal it really "put the fear of God" in all the other kids. This grouch looking doctor grabbed my arm about equal distance between my elbow and shoulder, swiped a little alcohol on a small spot and jabbed this mean looking needle into it without any warning. He didn't even tell me to turn my head, which would have been a big help. That arm swelled up, got feverish and ached for days - and nights. When all the other kids saw what a tragedy that was they sure didn't want any part of going to a doctor!

Me and a small percentage of whatever few kids I met up with were the only ones who'd had a shot, except for typhoid fever shots, which we got en masse at our schools, and we talked about it at great lengths like it had been triple by-pass heart surgery or worse.

Around our locale, we only knew of two kinds of doctors; one for sick people and the other a "tooth dentist." The only dentist we knew about practiced several miles from our house. Of course, a trip there took considerable time to plan and required cash on the spot for services rendered.

If our dad had a small tooth problem, like a tooth with sharp edges, or a mouth sore or an abscessed tooth, he handled it himself, even to pulling a few of them.

Neither the kids nor our mother ever entered a dentist's office unless they had a severe toothache of several days suffering. First, we tried our dad's remedy of cloves, then we tried the warm *poultices,* then we cried and complained long and loud and would not be comforted. At that time, our compassionate mother would persuade our dad we had to go get our tooth pulled.

Back then, the dentists didn't mess around with trying to save those teeth for future suffering, they just gave us a shot to deaden the feeling *a little,* took hold of some tooth extractors (or pliers), braced themselves, and gave a gargantuan yank. The tooth had no recourse; it did come out, sometimes accompanied by a few bone fragments, some of your gum flesh, and a lot of blood.

We sat in the dentist's office for a while and rinsed our mouths several times with cool water till most of the bleeding stopped, then we'd take a dampened handkerchief, pay the man his $1.00 and head for home. Sometimes we'd put our cleaned-up tooth under our pillow, from whence it got removed and a penny left in its place (our version of the Tooth Fairy).

This was our last experience with the "tooth dentist" till someone else developed a toothache and needed his tooth pulled. I don't remember if we ever got an infection from the wounded area, but we always survived, with the help of salt water rinses, and never did we even once think about going back to the executioner no matter what developed nor how long it took to heal.

Fun And Games
Homespun, Of Course

When I was a child we played things that our peers had played, and most of them were outside games that used real energy and ingenuity.

About the only thing we played where you sat down was "Pass the Thimble." At the right place and with the right folks, that was fun. It wasn't easy to guess who had the thimble if an ingenious kid did the passing.

Another "semi-still" thing that I enjoyed was drawing on the ground. To do this, you picked a smooth sandy surface and made it very smooth with your hand; then you'd get a stick and draw a person. You could erase (with your hand) their clothes and draw on new ones. Only one of my sisters would play this with me, and she couldn't draw too good. We had a little pet pig that always wanted to play but he didn't know where to step nor sit, so we just ran him off.

There were several sandy-yard games that we enjoyed. "Hop Scotch" was easy to learn and easier to do. The most skill required here was throwing the little broken piece of glass to just the right block. One that required the most concentration and ability was "Marbles." We had a great spot for playing that. It didn't please our mom to mess up her freshly swept front yard with all those little holes, but she'd rather have us out there playing than making noise and squabbling in the house. The fellers were much better marble shooters than the girls, but when we divided the sexes, us girls had a chance to win. Our poor fingernails sure took a beating scratching out those holes and making spans around them from which to shoot the marbles.

There was one game that could have been a little dangerous for us but we played it anyway. It was called "Mumble Peg." It required a 6"- 8" sharpish knife. We arranged the soft dirt in a mound, and then taking the bare-bladed knife, we went through all the rituals of the

12

game, using our palms for a springboard for bouncing the knife into place.

"Jack Stones" was played with five smooth yard pebbles and was a favorite of young and old. You needed to be pretty coordinated to handle all those stones. That was a long process completing all the steps to win the game. The present day "jacks" made of metal with a ball is a pushover. This was a game that was also handed down for generations.

We also had this thing we repeated and stirred a small stick around the "doodle bugs" house to make them come out. Their houses were little holes in the ground with a small mound of loose soil all around the top.

All of the other games were either standing or running or squatting, but definitely action games. One of the hardest and most unfair games was "Ante Over." You chose sides and threw the ball over a building, etc. That was all running and very tiring. Another similar game was "Knock the Tin Can" - whoever was "It" didn't stand a chance. The clever little kids hiding and knocking the cans sure gave "It" a workout for most part of an afternoon. There were no volunteers for the "It" - we just drew straws.

A lot of the games were dangerous; like climbing a young tree "sapling" and swinging over to the ground or to another tree or grabbing hold of a long elm tree limb and swinging across a gully or a ditch. Probably worse than that was sliding at breakneck speed down a steep hill covered with pine straw. Our slides were half-kegs, well greased. Two of us would sit on one and shove off with our feet down the steep hill between trees and around trees, guiding with our hand. The stopping place was on a steep bank of a creek.

Shooting a good homemade flip was not my forte. The most I could hit with my stone was my thumbnail. Some kids were quite accomplished with those "weapons", they could even kill a bird or a rabbit. Our parents were always on guard when they saw a kid with a flip. They didn't want any broken out window panes nor a head or eye injury.

A button on a string was a real fascinator. Often an adult would pick one up and see how long they could make them whir-r-r-r. As soon as a kid could get one started he'd entertain himself for hours.

There were also innumerable string tricks that we performed on our fingers. Each one had a name like making a "Jacob's Ladder," "Crow's Feet," etc. This took some expertise and concentration.

Our family really liked music, so we wasted a lot of time concocting noise makers. Things like tissue paper over a comb and blowing, also cornstalk fiddles, which we had to play on the outside because of the horrible screech. We also banged unmercifully on our old upright piano and strummed at great lengths on the old guitars and screechy violins. The howling dogs broke up a lot of our "concerts."

A girly game that was quiet and could take a long time was making a play churn. This needed a glass canning jar with fitted top, a hole punched in the top' and a small stick with a smaller stick nailed crossways. You had to fill the jar with water, add soap, screw on the top and churn till you were satisfied with the fine bubbles. It was great fun, and you could sing or recite poems (not poetry) as you churned.

When it was raining outside, our mother would let us use an old quilt and play "Mad Dog" with it. One person would be the mad dog and the others would huddle under the quilt and keep the edges tucked under so he couldn't get in. That was very exciting and sometimes hot.

We played a lot of "Dodge Ball" when we had enough room to draw a large enough oval ring. After playing a while we were pretty adept at dodging, so this game would often last a long time. My luck was to get in front of a slow kid and I couldn't dodge quick enough, so I'd get hit and get "out" the first thing. No girl's childhood was complete without a good, completely improvised play house. The only thing real was the imagination, rocks, planks, broken glass! Dirt, jar lids, bottles, and maybe moss. We often competed to see who could make the best play house, according to our mothers.

Just as important to boys were the cow pasture ball games. A good, hard stick or narrow plank sufficed for the bat, but you nearly had to have a real ball. Their hands were tough enough to catch and throw without a glove, luckily, and rocks served as base markers. If there were no cows around, it was fun for everyone except for times when a few fists were flying over unsolvable differences.

Cleaning The House And Yard

What was considered house cleaning years ago was quite different from what it is today. In the first place, the surfaces to be cleaned were different, the apparatus used and degree of cleaning were also. Only occasionally was there plaster or wallpaper and not even painted surfaces in some instances.

Most floors and walls were made of wood boards of various widths. The floors were often partially covered with a linoleum area rug. It was always so uplifting to get to buy a new floor cover after wearing the old one completely out in the center where all the heavy traffic was.

To repaint the walls was too expensive to consider, so we just washed them or swept them down. The yards were all sand or just plain dirt and we were careful to see that no grass grew on the pretty smooth sand. The only green things in the yard were shrubs, bushes, and a few flower beds.

For almost all house cleaning, removing cobwebs, knocking out wasp nests, banging on house bugs (flies, mosquitoes, roaches), sweeping the floors, removing dust in out-of-the-way places, or freshening up the chairs or sofas, the same 4-5 foot straw broom was used. These were made from tall straw that was collected in the low-lying lands that were not under cultivation, the blooms and rough straws were raked off with fork tines and bunched together with a strong cord about two feet to form a good handle. About 2 1/2 feet were left loose where the straw was small and loose on the ends to create the sweeping part.

They were very light and could be used with one hand and were real easy to help clean under the beds. They were also our mainstay for keeping the porches clean and came in handy for scaring the chickens off the porches or batting the cats off the cushions of the chairs.

Every house kept a good stock of broom straw on hand either in the Smokehouse or one of the other outhouses. If you couldn't gather it yourself, you could buy it from some of the blacks that often came by selling it or trading it for some edibles or old clothes.

It took forever to wash the windows and shutters. We only had soap and water for that job and it took a lot of rinsing and rubbing (with newspapers) to make the glass panes shine.

We used wide shuck mops for the floors, along with a little sprinkling of sand and lye soap to scour up all the greasy spots and the dirty, oily places on the porches where the hunting dogs insisted on sleeping. The rinse water was saved whenever possible to water the pots of flowers on the edge of the porches, often all the way around.

We saved all the old soft rags to dust with but often we'd wipe the furniture with a wet rag which deteriorated the varnished finish so badly that we'd have to repaint it. Some of the old furniture had as many as six coats of paint spread on it. The color it started out with soon got completely lost. We didn't have any long-range care in mind, just a temporary improvement.

It was always a dread when we had to take the lamps apart and wash those delicate glass chimneys and wash all the other glass objects that sat around. We could always think of a thousand things we would rather be doing. At intervals, our mother would make us take all of the chairs outside and scrub them. They sure looked better when we got through, but it was nothing to look forward to, especially with as many as we had and a mother looking over your shoulder to be sure you didn't skip a spot.

Almost all year round, we had to sweep those sandy yards to remove leaves, sticks, and chicken litter. We'd get two or three people together and make "rounds" sweeping. The first one in the row would make waves going in one direction, the second one would make them going in the opposite direction, then the third one repeated the first one's waves. When we had a lot of momentum built up, we were really synchronized. If you stooped over for any reason, you were likely to get your hair swept and a face full of sand. As soon as we'd finished sweeping with our perfect pattern of waves, we sure hated for anyone to walk across the yard and more so hated for the chickens to use them.

The brooms used for sweeping the yard were made of little tree or bush sprouts, tied together and limber so they would sweep and not scratch and be easier to use. These we had to gather in the Spring in a big supply, so they would last a while. We usually kept them in the corner of the back of the house or stored in some shelter nearby in a real handy place.

To complete the cleaning cycle, we had to burn the leaves and sticks that had accumulated around the edges of the yard. For this, we were ever mindful to keep a close lookout to prevent fire from spreading to one the shelter or outhouses. There was no playing allowed at one of these vigils.

Spring Planting

Anyone cursed with a poor family that was forced to raise cotton for a living deserves a throne of his own with a fan and a glass of iced tea in heaven.

Every spring, early in the season, our dad marched us to the community store and fitted us in a new straw hat and then just as carefully selected a new hoe for each of us - all to be paid for when we sold our cotton. Being as how they were something new we were proud of them for a few days.

The ensuing days brought out all the sure signs of springtime on the farm the smell of brush and corn stalks being burned, freshly plowed ground, which was kind of fun to walk on barefooted (since it was damp and cool), and a whole new set of names to call the poor old ornery mules.

With an ample supply of cotton and corn seed, guano, and the great urge of our dad to get on with the planting, everyone embarked on the spring ritual. Until the soil was prepared, we kids had a little play time in and around the fields. We'd eat green plums, scour the currant bushes for ripe or nearly ripe ones and scramble over the scratchy briars to pick a few dewberries or blackberries. Right in the middle of our fun our dad would yell for someone to go get some water. We'd rush home, draw a bucket of water and splash about half of it out trudging over the ditches and furrows to the men who were plowing. If there was any water left over after the men got a drink or two each, we'd sling it at each other with the dipper. This felt good, since the sun was scorching hot and there weren't many shady places.

Close to noon, the dinner bells would start ringing, and we knew instantly whose it was from the sound it made and the direction from which it came. Ours always sounded the best. At that tone, the men started unhitching the mules which made a bee-line for the barn, ready to eat, but they weren't nearly as accurate with their directions going back to work.

Whatever our mother found and concocted for lunch was good, and I guess every bite was eaten, but one thing was for sure: no one ate a bite till everyone was present and accounted for at the long banquet length table and the blessing had been asked. Our dad might not have adhered to other religious teachings, but that one made a lasting impression on him. Most of the time we had that ever refreshing "iced tea" for "dinner" (our noon meal).

Our old wood ice box kept a big chunk of ice for a while but as soon as it melted, one of us younger kids had to go to the store for another nickel's worth. That was a hot walk up a long hill, but with the ice melting all over you, it was much cooler coming back. There weren't many volunteers for this job unless the cotton was "eat up" with grass and we could take the time off from that chore.

As soon as we'd finished eating, or the food had run out, the girls would start clearing the table; all 12 plates, glasses, serving dishes, silverware, etc., and washing and drying and putting them all up ready for supper. Then it would be nap time. Most of us lay down for a few minutes for a rest of a sort. Some of us would lie down on the big porch, some of us would plop down on the double swing out in the yard, and the others would congregate in the wide hall that had open doors at each end.

When our dad had rested sufficiently he'd sound the call to bear arms and attack the fields one more time, but not without that final glass of iced tea that he'd saved on the buffet.

The heat was almost unbearable at this time of day and a breeze was almost non-existent, but as soon as our clothes were wet with sweat it seemed cooler, especially when we'd fan a little with those straw hats.

There were too many of us for everyone to be grouchy, so one or two in the bunch would think of something funny to tell or sing or do, and that would help to pass the time till about sundown, which was "praise the Lord" quitting time!

Going To Meetin

In our community you were strictly a "nobody" if you didn't go to church; and even worse, you never got invited out for dinner if you didn't go to church. Even though gossip was the neighborhood past time, the fact that you went to church put you on a pedestal right up there with the "gossip resistant."

Our household was definitely a divided house when it came to church membership. My mother was Baptist, without a doubt, but my father was Methodist or "hypocrite," as he put it. He loved the Bible when he was sober, but would quote scripture mostly when he was inebriated.

There was a Methodist Church in our community, but the Baptist Church was about six "dirt" miles away. Mostly we didn't have a vehicle that would run, and if we did, we didn't have a tag, and that wasn't necessarily illegal, but it was most unprestigious!!

Being a dozen of us, it was hard to fit even half of us in one automobile, so it was always a mystery who the *chosen* ones would be to make the next journey to the Baptist Church.

The most I can remember about the Baptist service, which was once a month, was the man who didn't know when to stop praying. He prayed for everybody and everything everywhere and repented for all his sins since the last month. Seems he only prayed once a month. I guess that he was the officially chosen prayer-giver. They had tried out another old man earlier and because he was shy or was a man of very few words, had passed this honor on to someone else. Once, when he was called upon to pray, he asked the congregation to stand and close their eyes, at which time he sneaked out of the service. There was a long pause of total silence before it was decided that someone else should lead the prayer of dismissal.

The Methodist Church was real close by, only about a mile from where we lived and almost every Sunday (weather fitting) we'd walk to Sunday School. There was also preaching Sunday once a month there, too.

As we'd walk along toward the church, other kids and occasionally an adult would join us till the road was about full and we'd kick up a lot of dust. By the time we got home we were good and dirty, even though we'd behaved ourselves; except for picking wild plums and blackberries on the sides of the road and just across the ditches.

There was an old pump organ in this church, and a really pudgy lady who loved satin dresses was the self-appointed organist. She wobbled all over the small stool which was completely hidden when she sat down, and we all enjoyed that immensely (that performance alone was well worth the trip).

The superintendent always read or "read at" the scripture printed in the Sunday school book. He was an unlearned man and had great difficulty reading in the Old Testament part. He'd read a few words and when he came to a word that was foreign or out of his vocabulary he'd insert "hard-word" and continue on to the next "hard-word." You didn't learn a lot, but it sure didn't take a long time to skim over those lessons either.

When the collection plate was passed, and I do mean *passed* - very little collection was ever taken, but this old man had an interesting ritual we all observed attentively. He'd dig around in his pocket as though the procedure was a surprise, then he'd take a few choice coins, squeeze them tightly, close his eyes and drop them into the collection plate (a typical "cheerful giver!"). On the way home, an occasional car would pass and stop to let us ride on the running-board. Now that was real class!!! All that cool breeze in your face and 5-10 miles per hour was much faster than some of us could walk.

We really looked forward to Sunday dinner, especially if the preacher *didn't* come home with us. That fried chicken and gravy sure let you know it was really

22

Sunday. The big 3 and 4 layer cake got wolfed down in a big hurry too; then we'd change our clothes, if we could find any, and go to the neighbors' house to play barnyard pasture ball or make a playhouse with the other kids.

Saturday P.M. Visitation

Nearly all the middle-aged women in our community were mothers. There were only about three single ladies that I recall, and they were definitely spinsters. One lady was married with no children, but she was an exception.

No one in that bracket dared to go visiting except on Saturday afternoon when the farm chores had been put aside till the next week and the housewives had cleaned house, washed the porches, swept the yards, and finished ironing for the week.

We usually ate an early lunch on Saturday and took our weekly baths early so we could put on our clean clothes and sit out on the porch and wait to see if anyone was coming, walking, down the hill toward our house. If not we started begging to go see our friends. If there were approaching guests, we were indeed happy to see them.

As soon as they got as close as the cemetery (about 200 yards away), the dogs would start barking and we'd get a broom and run them back under the porch. Then we would start getting fidgety, noticing the overhead spider webs on the ceiling of the porch or noticing the flower pots around the edge of the porch that were out of alignment, or dust on the chair rungs, or "whatever," but we didn't start working on them 'cause our visitors would see us; so we sat still till they were to our walkways' edge, and then we'd get up and start greeting them with "Hey, how are you feeling?" or "Ain't it hot!" or "That's a long pull ain't it?" Then we'd start complimenting them with, "That sure is a pretty dress," or "Your hair sure is pretty," or "How'd you hurt your toe!" if they were minus hose with a white rag around their toe (this was very common).

As soon as everyone had selected a seat we passed out our "funeral parlor" fans and everyone started rocking or swinging and fanning. The fans were dual purpose you could also bat gnats and flies with them. If the flies got real pesky, one of us would go get a swatter and start whipping on the flies.

24

The kids would usually, very slyly, sneak off the porch and out into the yard to play something while the adults sat there and talked about what little local gossip there was, then our mom would go get all her latest handmade things, like embroidery or quilt tops, or new pin cushions, or aprons, and show them off. As soon as everyone inspected each item and commented on how "pretty" they all were mom would go cut her weekend cake and open up some pickles and bring them out for everyone.

The kids had extra sensory perception about food, and when the cake was brought out we automatically came a running back to the porch. Some of the bigger kids were instructed to go get a cool bucket of water to pass around. As soon as the water had been passed around and everyone had taken a drink from the one dipper, my mom would suggest walking out to see her garden and the flowers and what new bushes or shrubs she had put out. Sooner or later, all the neighbors had the same plants and flowers cause they pinched off cuttings everywhere they went and took them home and coddled them till they were full-fledged plants. Anytime you walked out in the yard you had to look before you stepped, as we had chickens running around the yard, and they loved to mess up the good, freshly swept parts, where we mostly took our company.

After the garden inspection and the cuttings collected, it was usually getting time for the company to start leaving. This would often take another hour. There was no end to the "Ya'll come to see us," and just as they'd start walking off, one of them or my mom would think of something else to say or do and that would halt all operations. So, we'd go back to "We enjoyed the visit and Ya'll come again". Most of the time everyone had gone when the sun was about an hour high, just in time for us to go milk and get supper started.

New Dresses For The Girls

As surely as fall and spring came, our mother would dig out the Sears and Roebuck Catalogue where she'd study the new styles and colors for a few days, find all her old dress patterns of every size and shape and then make arrangements to go shopping for material.

It must have been an awful headache trying to keep enough clothes that fit for all of us. The boys and men's clothes were mostly store bought after about age 10. There was no way our mom could have sewed for us all, and the dresses didn't have to be tailored as much as the pants and shirts and jackets.

When my mother reached the place where she intended to purchase the materials she needed for her sewing, she'd go through a large stack of cloth before she'd make her final decisions about which prints and colors she needed for each child and how much cloth she'd need for each garment. During her decision making she had to keep in mind all the different girls hair and eyes colors, their ages and their particular likes in colors and styles. She also had to keep in mind who'd be wearing the dress later. Hand-me-downs was how our large brood was clothed.

After all of these considerations, she'd select two or three batches of material for each child. Of course she had to match buttons, threads, bias braid or ric- rac to the material and fairly often she'd buy some coordinating material to go with the figures or stripes to make collars or yokes for the outfits.

When she finally arrived home all tuckered out, she'd have an armload of fabric. We couldn't wait to get into it to see which ones were for us. A lot of the time, we could guess but occasionally more than one person would want the same piece of material. This led to a lot of compromising on everybody's part.

The very next day, we'd try to figure out who needed something new the worst, and mom would get out the pattern, make the necessary alterations and start cutting. Even though these clothes were customized, you couldn't return them if they didn't fit, which was somehow the case; however, we were so anxious to wear them, we didn't even notice an ill fit for the most part.

Sometimes we'd fling such a fit about the necks being too big or the waist too wide, that she'd have to do some parts over. If they wound up too short, she'd just add a wide border to the bottom of the skirt. She never did lack for remedies.

Our mother was kind of artistic about matching things up and even though she had to use the same patterns over and over, she'd improvise and come out with a fairly attractive dress. We nearly always got compliments on our new frocks and of course, they turned out to be our favorites. Sometimes we'd even wear that same one two days in a row. The sewing machine was kept busy till all that new material got used up. Some days our mom would make a whole dress in one day and even get another one started. Back then, there were no zippers so all of the openings, front or back, had buttons. Often making the button holes took about as long as making the rest of the garment.

Some of the older girls learned the *art* and that helped out a lot. They also helped with the hemming. Luckily, we didn't have any "pot bellies" and not too many "sway backs" so the hems were easy to turn up and usually looked even when we tried them on.

Nearly all the dresses had sashes and they stayed torn off about half the time, cause they were perfect for grabbing kids with, also they got caught on a lot of things and untied themselves making them easy to tear off. Nothing was quite as tacky as a straggly headed kid with droopy stockings and untied sash. The kids "bugged" the daylights out of the bigger ones to tie their sashes.

For our mom, all of the "before school days" were spent cutting and sewing, her back must have been awfully tired. She'd sew a while, hop up and grab something to eat, and sit right back down to her sewing. As soon as we saw what she had to eat we'd want something to eat just like hers. That was a big hindrance, but at least she could rest her eyes for a little while.

On occasions she'd use up all the material for a certain dress and lack just a little bit more. She'd send one of us to the store with a sample for some additional fabric. If the storekeeper had sold out of that piece, he'd send a substitute. At first our mom would be furious, but then she'd set about working the unmatched material in with a little ric-rac or bias tape in between. Most of the time it looked all right till it was washed and a few colors ran.

When everyone was finally outfitted in all those dresses there weren't many days of reprieve for our mom, since she also had to make some of those famous homemade bloomers, slips and a whole batch of warm nightgowns.

Saturday Grooming

After a week of hard work we really needed some time for grooming. Our poor hands looked terrible, our faces sun-parched, hair scraggly and feet all dried out, but, with a lot of help we perked them all up a bit for Sunday or an occasional date on Saturday night.

We got up bright and early and kept a fire going in the stove so we could keep our irons hot and tackled the ironing. This was menial labor and took a long time. Most of our clothes were made of cotton or rayon and both had to be ironed at just the right temperature. As soon as we'd cleaned off our *very* hot irons we'd iron the cotton things first and as soon as the irons cooled off some we'd iron the rayon things. Then we'd have to press the men's blue serge pants with a press cloth; these seldom got cleaned, just pressed over and over at home.

The next thing on our priority list was the baths and hair washing. As soon as we'd drawn enough water for both we'd get those two chores underway. Since shampoo was not a word in our vocabulary, we "washed" our hair, which was the way it was. Octagon soap was the main cleaner we used, and it made your hair shiny, especially with a little vinegar in the rinse water.

Most of us girls had straight hair and that was a real problem; we thought only curly hair was pretty, so we strained our brains to concoct some curls or waves. To make the curls last we'd sometimes use sugar water and little rags to wind the hair up. Often the sugar water made the hair a little whitish looking in places but the flies liked it. When this method didn't work we'd use those crimping irons that were heated over a glass lamp chimney. Your hair got burned and singed after several settings but at least it wasn't poker straight.

After a few years the style switched to finger waves. Only a few of the more accomplished hair dressers could perfect this style. One of my sisters was greatly in demand for this new coiffure. Our neighbors came from all around for this front porch beauty treatment. One of

29

them had extremely thick hair and it had been miserable for her, so she thinned it herself. This she accomplished by holding the hair up on top of her head and shaving all the hair underneath. She also came to get her hair finger-waved!? We all had to excuse ourselves to go off and laugh after which my "finger-waving" sister commenced to try to fix it. The pins and waves just fell down because they had nothing to hold them in place. Most pretty afternoons in the spring and summer were completely used up fixing everyone's hair. The young girls all had the same haircut; not with a soup bowl but not much better. The bangs were chopped off well above the eyebrows so you wouldn't need them trimmed so often. The guys all got sheared by our local self-appointed barber, with no formal training, who operated in the back of our dad's general merchandise store, the same place you could buy fresh mullet.

Jergens lotion was at a premium at our house, cause it provided all the skin care we knew anything about. We used it for face cream for years, with a scant amount for our hands. Sometimes our heels were so rough we'd grease them good with tallow (made from beef fat). After this treatment we'd have to sit around with our feet hoisted for a long time to let that grease dry in so as not to track up the floors with the stuff.

There were a few store bought aids that the grown girls used, such as face powder, Maybelline eyelash enhancer, and lipstick. These were kept under lock and key so us younger kids couldn't get into them and waste them. They were used only when one of the older girls had a date or was going off to a party, or visiting, or to church. We certainly could have used the improvements, but those items were too expensive to be used for the whole family's benefit.

Catching The School Bus

The really dreaded age in the kids' lives was being old enough or being promoted out of grammar school and having to catch the school bus for high school.

Some of the parents and county officials thought they had wrought the miracle of the century when they got the school bus system worked out for our area, but some of the kids were finding out otherwise.

At this time the buses were another form of big truck, not warm, nor very cool, plank seats running the full length of the bus with nothing to hold on to as we bumped over the rough roads and swerved around the curves. Kids would often land on the floor or flop all over each other or grab onto whatever was close by to hang on to and stay in place.

The windows would never work right, if you got one down, it wouldn't go back up and often we'd get rained on or frozen half to death. In real bad weather, things were even worse. First you got wet waiting for the bus (they didn't operate like trains) then you squeezed by all the other kids on the bus and got them wet. No one wanted you to sit by them, so they'd spread out all kinds of ways so you had a hard time trying to find somewhere to sit. If it took very long to find a seat the driver would drive off with a jerk and sling you right down in someone's lap. The big ruts in the road made it even harder for the driver to hold the bus between the "bar ditches" plus there was always this dreaded threat of getting stuck or sliding into a ditch.

Occasionally a bus would break down en route to school and this caused all kinds of problems; not much traffic on the roads and houses far apart with very few telephones, so we'd get to sit there for hours with no help in sight. The kids would get restless and ornery and even start fighting, which was popular in those days. The bus drivers were usually real mild mannered and had little control over a situation of that caliber.

There was really no wonder that we kids made up all kinds of excuses to miss school. There were no truant officers and some of our parents were real lenient about letting us stay home.

In the first place, it was hard to get up early enough to catch that bus in the winter months and half of the time we didn't have our homework done along with we didn't like what we had to wear, or we had a bad cold and couldn't find a clean handkerchief or our lunch wasn't to our liking. There were all kinds of excuses for missing the bus; one of our favorites being, "We had developed an upset stomach at the last minute."

Often when we got on the bus, we'd have a special place we wanted to sit between two of our friends and there'd really be no room, so we'd wedge ourselves in anyway shuffling our fannies from side to side making room. The kids above and below sure didn't like it, but they did the same thing on other occasions.

We had one idiot driver who would actually wait for us at the main road. It was a very short distance from our house, but we'd poke around, leave a notebook or pencil and have to go back for it or we'd just plain get up late and not be dressed when the bus came. Don't remember all the gory details about what happened when we finally arrived at the school house and made our way to our rooms after the bell had rung.

Most of us thought we were born with enough smarts and there was no real reason to go to school. On the other hand, the basketball players or relay runners could hardly wait to get there.

It was kind of difficult finding the right bus to get on in the afternoons. They all looked alike and were parked in a different place every afternoon so if the drivers had left the buses to go smoke, we'd often get on the wrong bus. When it was decided which kid belonged on which bus, the right one would sometimes be gone. A kid without a bus was a fate worse than death. Some parents were extremely hard to get in touch with.

Not only were the buses for school kids (aged 12-21), it also served as a commuter service for some of the "no car" adults. These grownups would hail the bus, climb on and state their destinations and crawl off with a "much obliged" and in a few days, or the same afternoon, board again for that free ride. It wouldn't have ·mattered much except they always wanted to sit at the end of the seat at the front of the bus and that meant we had to crowd and shove and wiggle all the way to the back in order to make room for them.

The entire seventh grade graduating class-
Including the teacher.

School Daze

Our little community was apparently *very prosperous* when I was a kid, cause we had a "two-room" schoolhouse with a "backhouse" that would accommodate three people at a time. The "Little Room" of the schoolhouse was for "primer" age kids through third grade, and the "Big Room" was for all the others (four through seven). There was only one teacher per room, but the discipline was for real, cause if you got reprimanded or spanked at school, you got a bigger one when you got home. There were no sassy nor disrespectful kids.

Our school had that famous ole pot-bellied stove for heat, and everyone shoved their desks as close to it as they could without scorching their clothes. Usually the first thing on the agenda was the "roll call," and it was answered with a Bible verse. Most days were "God is love" or "Jesus Wept," but for a few occasions we'd learn a new verse and blurt it out loud and clear, much to the teacher's surprise. I liked to learn new ones, so often I'd come out with something different but authentic. One little girl, very pretty and sweet but not too scholastically inclined, asked me for a verse. On the spur of the moment, I wasn't that learned about the Bible, but without hesitation I whispered to her, "Grease the cup." She very trustingly yelled out, "Grease the cup" when the teacher called her name. The other kids didn't know the difference, but the teacher asked her to repeat it. She obliged, at which time the teacher turned her head and lost her composure.

The first classes in the morning were usually reading. When you'd heard all the different stories, corrections, and lack of proper pronunciation from the fourth (really the second grade level) through the seventh grades, you were fit to be tied. It's no wonder we made and threw spitballs at each other at random and wrote notes and passed them all over the room. Of course, if you were caught at either, they carried a stiff penalty; at least sitting in a corner with a dunce cap on.

There were a few kids who could really read, except they had no idea as to feeling or expression, and it was such a sing-song, nasal exercise you couldn't tell when one sentence started and another ended, so much so that the teacher once asked the next kid to "sing."

The spelling bees or classes were my favorites. For some reason, spelling was easy for me. For an innocent observer, these classes would have been a hoot. A lot of kids simply could not spell, and their efforts were hardly related to the correct spelling.

Math was especially hard for most of us, for we had no one who would help us with our homework, and the poor teacher didn't have enough time to spend with each child. I think I was half through high school before I learned the multiplication tables and almost as old before I mastered the alphabet, especially when I tried to figure out what letter followed when you'd stop in the middle of the alphabet.

Recess was by far the only thing we looked forward to. However, due to the wide range of ages and sizes of the kids, it was difficult to play a game you were interested in. The little kids were always in the way of the big kids, and as soon as we'd really get into a game of "hide and seek" or "dodge ball," the bell would ring, and we'd have to line up to march back into our room.

As soon as we all got seated, about five hands would fly up with the kids wanting to be "excused" to go to the toilet. They didn't want to waste their recess or lunch time for that purpose. The teacher was irate but didn't dare to refuse the request.

Lunch time was nothing to look forward to. Some of us went home for lunch, some of us brought our lunch. At any rate, the lunches were almost always the same whatever was left from breakfast, plus an occasional baked potato or slice of cake or cookie. There was one little girl whose parents let their sausage hang in cloth bags all year, and the mother would make fresh biscuits every morning to go with it. She also made super gingerbread with icing on top and filled the little girl's lunch box with these goodies. Whenever we could swap with her or con her out of her lunch we thought we'd hit the jackpot.

When we went home for lunch, we'd hurry down the hill and back, so we could get in a little "hop scotch" or "jump the rope" (a vine). When the wind was blowing hard in our faces we'd sometimes walk backwards up the hill. One day it was very cold, and I pulled my knitted cap over my eyes. I must have headed out in the wrong direction, cause I walked right squarely into a ditch full of cold, cold water. When I got to the schoolhouse I was as wet as a rat. The teacher made me sit real close to the heater to try to get dried off in time to go home.

The thing that all of us really looked forward to was getting ready for the Christmas program. For this event our parents were allowed to come to school with us and see us perform. Each kid, no matter how shy or stupid, was given a "recitation." The girls usually got the longest poems, cause the boys didn't want one at all, and the teacher had learned from past experience that the girls did much better.

The kids' ages ranged from five to fourteen, and often a kid about 3 1/2 feet tall would be placed by a strapping big old farm boy, clad in farm attire that made him look like a man, to render their Christmas speeches.

First off, an older girl would come hurrying out on the stage, face all flushed, and recite her welcome speech before she got to the designated spot. With her hands securely behind her back, swinging from side to side in tempo with the rhymes, she'd wall her eyes to the top of her head and get through with it. This really made everyone feel welcome and all the other kids nervous.

On the stage behind the kids was a huge cedar tree with scant trimmings, but this one was special! At other times the only adornment in the room was the dreaded blackboard. Almost every year we had these big cardboard letters that spelled Christmas being held by children who had memorized a rhyme to go with them.

They were really interesting and *advanced*. They went
something like this:

C -   is for Christmas - the best time of the year
H -   is for holly - to bring us good cheer
R -   is for reindeer - to pull Santa's sleigh
I -   is for icicles - to brighten the day
S -   is for Santa - all dressed up in red
T -   is for toys - for Reba and Ted
M-   is for music - so merry and gay
A -   is for apples - you need one a day
S -   is for soot - in the chimney so black...
We hope that next year you all will come back.

The next major event was Valentine's Day. We kinda'
dreaded that one, cause it was hard to find enough cards
to go around. We kept our cards from year to year,
erased the names of previous senders and gave them out
again till the erased spots made a hole in the cards.
When this supply was exhausted we'd set about making
some by hand from various and sundry paper materials,
using those original and brilliant verses that always
started out with "Roses are red , .. , etc," - we finished out
the list, teacher and all.

The girls were always embarrassed when a boy gave
them a valentine. The teasing that usually followed was
unbearable and went on all through school. After
Valentine's Day, the weather was bad and colds and flu
and even pneumonia were rampant. Absenteeism was
very high till spring weather opened up and shortly after
that the farmers had to have the children to help with the
planting, so there were very few children in school.

It's good that there were no state or national tests that
had to be passed, otherwise some of us would still be
there trying to learn those multiplication tables or the
basic reading skills.

Whether To Stay Home Or Go

As seldom as we got to go anywhere in a car it seemed we would all want to go whenever the word was mentioned. But that wasn't necessarily the case. We had this older sister who was a good babysitter and was often left in charge of the group that had to stay home. This was very much to our liking, for she really knew how to entertain when the parents weren't there.

She'd make syrup candy with peanuts, if there were any, or cook a cake complete with sugary icing - all of which had to be eaten in its entirely before the parents returned. These were some of the treats that gave us second thoughts about going away.

Once when pecans had just started to ripen and open we gathered all we could by the usual method of pulling down limbs and picking or poking them out of their shells, when we decided someone should climb up the tree and shake or stomp on the limbs to make a few more nuts fall. As soon as the person was chosen and she had managed to climb up the tree, with a little help from her friends, she started shaking and stomping the limbs. One hefty stomp was a little too much, and it started one of the limbs to cracking. She managed to get off that one, but it came breaking down to the point where we decided we'd better pool our strength and pull it down and hide it, or our parents were sure to give us all a whipping. As soon as we dragged the large limb off and hid it in our deep gully, we noticed it had left a considerable white scar - very obvious. After much thought and exchanging of ideas, we came up with the idea of getting soot from the chimney, mixing it with a little water and painting over it. That turned out to be a good idea that lasted several weeks and no one was the wiser till our dad found the broken limb in our hiding place.

On another occasion in the spring, when the small apples were about the size of marbles or small eggs, our parents would caution us not to pull the green apples. Well, we didn't; but we weren't long figuring how we could hold an apple with one hand and eat the apple while still on the limb, or we'd knock them off so we could say we didn't pull them. Those little sour balls with salt sprinkled on them were something else!

At other times, when the weather was warm, but before May (which was the official barefoot time), as soon as the parents were out of sight we'd take off our shoes and go barefooted. For this misbehavior we were rewarded with a fresh cold or a sore throat and no one had to guess twice where we got them. In some cases I guess the parents had mixed emotions about leaving home too.

Reading Material

On our farm there was nothing much to read and even less time for reading. In our area very little time was spent reading. Most people were very slow readers and unusual words presented a problem, we didn't know the correct pronunciation, much less what they meant; so we really didn't enjoy it.

We felt the need and an obligation to read the Bible. Some people made that a practice on a regular basis while others read it on occasions, especially during or right after the summer revivals or "August Meetings," as we called them. (The name being derived from the time they were held). It was a must for the kids to memorize the books of the Bible. I don't know how that came to be so important, but it seemed like more emphasis was placed on that than on what the books contained.

Probably next to the Bible, in importance, was the Grier's Almanac. No household was complete without one. It was kept close by for fast reference (mostly in the kitchen). The elders all knew about those signs, the stars, the moon locations, the sky colors, clouds, and everything else pertaining to nature. That almanac contained everything that was necessary for a farmer to know. From it he could tell when and how to plant his garden and crops, he even knew when it was supposed to snow. If the corn husks or animal fur or height of corn didn't reveal the fierceness of the succeeding seasons, he could always refer to the almanac.

Everyone on the rural route with a mailbox got one of those "market bulletins". My dad even "hunted" his eyeglasses to read it from "Cover to Cover." If on one of his trips to the store he heard an interesting thing that someone else had read and he had missed it, we'd have to retrieve ours from wherever we'd put it to let him read it for himself. That publication and its contents was one thing the whole neighborhood had in common. Some of our neighbors saved every edition, but we just used ours in the best manner, such as lining kitchen shelves, shining window panes, starting fires, or as toilet paper.

The most anticipated printed material for us was the Sears & Roebuck catalog. We'd do without food to get to order a few things so we'd be sure to receive one the next year. It took a long time for each of us to thumb through all of those pages and wish for and dream about owning all of those tempting items ranging from "Sunday, Goin' to Meeting Clothes," to cooking utensils, to farm equipment and everything in between. They must have weighed 15 pounds and were generally referred to as "The Wish Book."

Our mother would order several items all along but about half of the time, she'd have to return them for one reason or another. Our dad's country store was the source for most of our clothes and real needs, but we had neighbors who did most of their buying from their catalogs. The place where we most enjoyed "The Wish Book" was at the toilet. We'd sit on those hard boards with that book all to ourselves in the quiet and privacy of the "outhouse" and go back over those pages time and again, not once tiring of all those wonderful items and colorful pictures. Sometimes we'd save the prettiest pages of ladies and children's clothes, with real people modeling them, for paper dolls.

The real reason for the catalog's being there in the first place was to be used for toilet paper. It, along with a few county newspapers, served a dual purpose, entertainment included.

Our county paper let us know what people in the surrounding communities were doing. Some had been visiting, some dying, some had a few things to sell, and some had moved. Many items such as homemade soap, dried apples, all kinds of seeds. little pigs, tombstones, kindling, and firewood, etc., could be bought from the ads in the paper.

It also touched on the happening at the county seat. New restrictions or laws that had been passed, where the next singing would be held, when and where they'd give the next typhoid shots, and a little other pertinent information. We seldom subscribed to that paper but our nice neighbor read hers and passed it on to us.

One other way of keeping in touch with the rest of the world, or next community, was with the little bit of correspondence that went on.

My mother would receive letters from her family that lived in other counties but they were seldom very news noteworthy nor informative. They'd usually start off with "As I have nothing else to do" and continue on to say we are "very well," along with telling what the spring garden status was and how many little chickens they had "taken off" as well as all the other important home matters. Only rarely did anyone receive any earth-shattering news like "Lem broke his leg" or "Uncle Mathias died" or "Zeke's mumps fell on him." Every now and then, they'd include a new recipe or a pretty picture that was on a last year's calendar - suitable for framing.

There wasn't much mail that got delivered to our house. It's no wonder stamps stayed three cents for so long. The most activity that our postman encountered, except for when Sears & Roebuck sent out their yearly catalog, was transporting people all over the community and carrying "free of charge" hand written notes to neighbors, sometimes in exchange for sweet potatoes or eggs.

I can't remember any magazines from way back then, not that there weren't any. I guess those salesmen knew that it would be futile to travel so far from town, plus the hardship of traveling over such rough terrain.

From some unremembered source, we had acquired a few real books. Some old Shakespearean Classics, which may as well have been written in Latin, some poetry from Burns, completely indecipherable, some old unheard of brand of encyclopedias, and a few old frayed-back books of a sort that only collected dust at our house. The only time we opened up an encyclopedia was from complete boredom. Occasionally, we'd happen up on a picture or some information that made an impression, but unfortunately this was on rare occasion.

Chicken Raising

Chickens which were supposed to be raised for eating, egging, and raising other chickens also served another worthwhile purpose. They had built-in time mechanisms that sounded off each and every morning at the same time (akin to an alarm clock), and often they'd announce sundown and midnight as well. They ate unsightly scraps that had been flung out the back door; they debugged some of the vegetables and helped to rid the yard of those wiggly worms.

All of their abilities and talents weren't necessarily good ones, however. They were notorious for coming up the steps on to the porch and using the nice clean wooden plank floors for a rest room. They pecked on the apples (as they fell to the ground) which would ordinarily be used to make applesauce; also, a lot of the garden vegetables were ruined by pecks if there were no fences around the garden. But their favorite spot was right in the middle of a cherished flower bed wallowing and scratching the loose dirt or dust. You could hear all the neighbors far and wide hollering, "Shooooo!" at the wayward ones, scaring them off the porches and out of flower beds.

Mostly, they were good natured critters, except for an occasional ill-tempered ole rooster or an old setting hen whose inclination was to "set" (meaning to cover eggs with her body till the 'lil chickens hatched). They raised Adorable offspring, which, luckily, didn't look like their moms nor pops till they were almost grown.

It was always interesting to watch the mother hen take care of her chicks. They were real responsive to the mother hen's "clucks." The mothers and young were kept together in a triangular coop with wood slats about an inch or so apart. We poked their food and water in there for a few days and then we'd turn them out. The chicken hawks were a constant worry for those mothers, because they would come out of nowhere, dive down, and in spite of ole mother hen's defenses, grab up a baby chick with their claws and flyaway. Our father kept his shot gun loaded to handle this situation, but the hawks seemed to know when he wasn't around. It took a lot of calling, feeding, and scaring off and cleaning up to finally get them to the point where you could really enjoy them on the table.

In preparation for eating, they first had to be "coop fed" for several days, then the official "chicken plucker" caught a good plump one by the leg, dragged him out of the coop and wrung his neck. If you weren't experienced at this job you'd bungle it, and your chicken, which was supposed to be dead would hop up and wobble off in a lop-sided stride. As soon as they were pronounced dead they were scalded, defeathered, and dressed and made ready for frying. These young, plump, tender and delicious critters were the favorite of family, friends, associates, and especially preachers. But no one dared to serve them without gravy and hot biscuits. It was a short but active life for the chickens.

Slopping The Hogs

Every farmer had one to four pigs which he fattened one way or another for his own personal eating and sharing with his neighbors, and no matter where he went for the day all roads led to home in time to "slop the hogs" before dark. We kids loved the little pigs and wanted to let them run loose in the yard for pets. They were extremely friendly and much smarter than a two-toed sloth.

Don't know why we always said "slop the hogs." Sometimes they were only pigs, but the food was always the same and with good luck the pigs did turn into hogs. Whoever named the process of feeding them "slopping the hogs" sure hit the nail on the head. 'T'was indeed a sloppy mess and a sloppy job.

All of our table scraps (except bones) and peels of every sort and other discarded food from every source along with the dishwater after we'd washed the dishes went into a large pail which we called the "slop bucket." This mess we saved from morning 'til night to take to the pigs.

The big open top pail was kept near the stove or table where we washed the dishes and there was the ever present danger of dropping a hot pad or dish towel in there. On one occasion a small kid fell in one of them head fist but was quickly rescued even though he didn't smell so good. This pail came in real handy when you got a hold of something you didn't like to eat cause no one knew what it was later, nor who discarded it. We got pretty adept at throwing things even across the room into the slop, although it did spatter the floor a little. Of course we had to clean it all up as soon as it was discovered.

When the big pail got over half full, someone would have to carry it to the hog pen to empty it. The sloppy foul smelling stuff would literally slop up on you as you trudged along, getting to the pen. The pens were always built away from the house on a downgrade so the wind would not blow the odor back to the house.

Someone finally decided to make a big trough that had a shoot from the outside where you poured the food concoction (a big improvement over stomping around in the pens up to your ankles in pig manure).

If the slop looked too thin, we had to supplement the feed with corn, half-rotted apples that had fallen off the tree, bad peaches, tiny sweet potato roots with vines, peanut vines and various and sundry other plants and at times we'd even boil squash in a big black pot on the outside to add to their food.

There was no way those hogs were going hungry for very long as Mother Nature had endowed them with a shrill squeal that carried a long way and wouldn't shut off until they made you aware of their needs, which always meant more food!

When you had time to observe them eating and the odor wasn't too offensive, It was entertaining to watch them dunk those long snouts into the food and look up and grunt their approval or dislike for what you had given them. If there were more hogs than one, they'd nuzzle each other over to be sure they were in the best spot and were getting the most food; hence, the old saying "ate like a hog." At the very best, their manners were extremely rude, their abodes good and messy, their attire thickly cruddy and their appetites insatiable. So why not just "feed 'em slop."

When all was said and done and they were properly cared for, the ham and sausage and pork chops and spareribs that they produced sure meant tasty eating. For such to come from those foul-looking and smelling varmints was certainly one of the millionth wonders of the world.

Seven Maids A Milking

For as long as I can remember our milk cows were almost like family. Milk was a very important part of our diet and everyone in our community had at least one milk cow.

Just as sure as the sun rose and set we (along with our neighbors) were out at the barns bellowing "S o o o o o o Cow, S o o o o o o Cow," for as long as it took to get all the cows up for milking.

At our house that job got handed down from mother to daughter to another girl as soon as they became 10 or 12 years old. Seems the men and boys were immune to this job. Few and far between were the ones eager to learn the art.

As soon as we got the cows assembled, we'd take the feed and dole it out, take our milk pails with a little water in the bottom for washing the teats, find our usual spot and squat down or kneel, or in some cases, sit on a small stool and start the milking. Our Mother sat on an old "slop jar" turned upside down to milk, that was just the right height.

The milking itself wasn't so bad in nice weather. It was the rainy days that created the problems. In and around the barn was squish, stinky dirt mixed with manure, and you really had to be careful where you stepped so as to avoid sliding down or messing up your feet.

The old cow's tail stayed full of cockleburs, and when it got good and wet, it made a nasty whip. Even though the tail was for swatting flies and bugs, the ole cow would eventually wind up smacking you in the face at least two or three times while you were trying to milk. Often we'd smack her back, but not too hard lest she stepped in our milk pail and ruined the milk or scraped our leg or foot with her sharp hoof.

With the tail as bad as it was, that was not our most dreaded thing; her breath was even worse. With those wild onions and bitter weeds both to contend with we really needed a surgical mask. If your pasture ever got bitter weeds in it they were there for life. Fortunately the cows only ate it when it was young and tender. But the wild onions they ate with everything as long as it was green. The wild onions took root in China and you simply could not pull them all up. You could hardly dig them up either, and worse than anything, they made the milk (and butter) taste horrible.

Our Mother tried hard not to have to use the night's milk when the cows had been eating onions, but with a family the size of ours we were forced to use some of it. During these times our Dad would send us out to cut Johnson grass to feed them to help dilute the bad taste.

The cats were always a problem around the milk pails. Their keen sense of smell led them directly to the source of their favorite beverage. Being the kids that we were, we'd aim the milking teat at the cats and squirt milk to them; or we'd spray another kid who was standing around. Of course this practice was never indulged in when the parents were in sight.

Most people called their milk cows "Bossy," and every one who ever milked a cow knew why. If she parked in a bad place for you to milk her you'd have to shove and push and bang on her for eons to get her to move. She'd use her tail on you if you got too rough, or she'd take off in the opposite direction and you'd really have a problem trying to coax her back to the proper place.

The ole "heifers" had a built-in time system about being fed or milked. It worked real good on average length days, but when summer and winter came along it got fouled up, and if you thought you were gonna milk at 6:30 it was just a fantasy. You milked when "Ole Bossy" decided to amble up to the barn. No amount of "S o o o o o Cowing" made much difference. She just kept on grazing and chewing her cud till it suited her to do otherwise.

If we had a date or somewhere to go on the weekends we'd go to the backside of the pasture and drive her up to try to get the milking over with.

At intervals, the cows would "dry up" or stop giving milk and we were always jubilant to have that occur. Of course, it wasn't very long before they calved and had to be milked as before - only worse. Trying to separate the cow and calf was a whole new battle!

In Search Of A Turkey Nest

Turkeys are indeed some of nature's weirdest varmints. They look kinda ordinary, but ours weren't. The old Toms that we had hated people. As soon as we'd go to the well to draw a bucket of water, he'd start his attack. Seemed as if he knew we'd have both hands busy with the water bucket operation and couldn't clobber him with anything but a foot, and he could easily dodge that. So, he always came a-running when we let the bucket down in the well. Our Mother wouldn't let us knock his head clean off, which is what we all wanted to do, for she needed him around so she could raise some babies.

We didn't like turkey meat in the first place, and knowing the tortuous task of finding the eggs to be hatched, we weren't enthused about any of it. The mother turkeys were a powerfully suspicious lot. They could walk looking backwards to be sure we were or weren't following them. They never ever built a nest close to our house; in fact, the further away they could make it the better they liked it.

Sometimes they'd travel three or four miles away. These gangster-minded ole rascals would lead us everywhere but to a straight shot to their nests. I'm sure they had researched the perfect area for their precious eggs. One trail that led through a neighbor's pasture was the "stomping ground" of the dreaded neighborhood bull.

When our Mother decreed that we were to trail the turkey hens, we immediately donned our worst clothes and found the hoe and an axe. This was gonna be a dual purpose trip. En route we always located some slim dogwood sprouts which we cut down and brought home for "brush brooms" (these were used to sweep our sandy yards). A lot of times we ran across broom sage, from which we made our house brooms. So we were keeping all this in mind when we were leaving on one of these four to five-hour trips.

First, we ran the obstacle course of squishing through a real wet, miry spot near the branch. From there we trailed off into the cotton fields, where we always picked up a few cockleburs and beggar lice. The little cotton wisps left in the rotten bolls were the perfect beggar lice removers, but the cockleburs had to be removed by hand one at a time. Each one added a new pricked place on your fingers.

Next, we'd cross the road and head toward that famous pasture (where the fierce neighborhood bull resided). The turkeys always looking back to make sure they weren't taking the long route for nothing. At the fence's edge we'd take turns holding up the barbed wire for each other and undoing the clothes that had gotten caught on the sharp barbs (adding a few more scratches to the fingers).

We were so afraid of seeing that ole bull we could hardly keep our minds and eyes on watching the turkeys. Once we had surmounted that problem we cleared the other side of the fence to a purely wooded area where the brush brooms were. We'd pause long enough to chop down some of those sprouts and proceed with them in our arms to wherever else our feathered friends led us. Needless to say, we did spot a number of snakes along the way, but they were just as afraid of us, so they slithered out of the way.

Sometimes the turkeys would wander out of the way to get a drink of water. This also gave us a chance to rest. From our experience in years past this would be close to the nesting grounds. At this point, we'd hold back and sit down to appear not to be watching. The turkeys would sneak off and go a little further to a really thickly concealed spot, lay their eggs, attempt to cover their nests and start homeward.

We had been instructed to gather all the eggs and bring them home. We had gone prepared to carry them, so this was no problem, except hurrying back through that ole cow pasture. It's a wonder we got back with whole eggs after all that jolting. But, once we were back we didn't have to worry about that ordeal till the next spring. We just concentrated on dodging ole Tom every time we needed to draw water and thinking up some way to get rid of that plagued meat on Thanksgiving and Christmas.

The Call Of The Wild
(Ripe Blackberries)

Every parcel of untended ground on our farm was covered in briars from which we gathered those much sought after blackberries. They were both a blessing and a curse. The curse being the ever-grabbing long vines covered with strong sticky briars. They'd attack you from great distances (surely a cousin to the Venus Flytrap).

Almost every year these vines were in full production, the weather very seldom froze them out nor did the blights destroy them. They came up and grew all by themselves, the only other thing they needed was, as one farmer put it, "Laziness." With all the hard long hours it took to grow the crops and gardens, one simply did not have the strength to battle those vines that grew so abundantly.

Our family loved blackberry jam, jelly, juice, pies, or anything else you could make from them and there weren't many barriers that kept us from picking them. In the latter part of May or June, or early July, we kept a sharp vigil for those blossoming vines to start putting on berries and then for them to start ripening. It was hard to tell which was most important at that season, either chopping, hoeing, and thinning the cotton, or picking the blackberries. For either task all the paths led by one "busting-open" peach tree. These were early, little, yellowish, free-stone jewels that we gorged ourselves on.

Our dad insisted that the cotton came first, after all, he owed a lot of money that he had borrowed to be paid back when we sold our cotton, so he had a lot riding on that cotton crop. Our mother, who was about eighth in command, was dead-set on gathering a big harvest of berries, so we were really kept busy trying to get it all done.

My mother, with the help of a smaller kid or two, would open up the season. She'd round up all the necessary garb: strong clothes, a hat, gloves (usually frayed dress

52

gloves that had been discarded), tough shoes (also some which were not good enough to wear anywhere else - old, worn ones revived with a couple of layers of cardboard, so the rocks couldn't punch through the holes so easily), a bucket (so we could hang the handle over our arm and leave the hands free for picking), and one hoe. A good hoe was necessary for knocking down bushes or weeds and running off or killing snakes, which we always encountered either in the vines or en route.

It was really exciting to come up on some vines that were literally covered in clusters of berries. We'd dive in with a bunch of gusto till those strong, briared vines would reach out and grab your sleeves or pants legs and it was real difficult to get them to turn loose. When you'd dislodge one sleeve, the idiot vine would grab you in the back, while another would reach over and snatch your hat off. They sure tried your patience, however, we were so determined to go home with a big load of berries that we just ignored all the harassment.

We'd pick a while, compare amounts, and then take out a few, blow 'em off real good, and eat' em. When we'd catch our comrades not looking, we'd sneak a few out of their pails so we could brag about having the most.

There were an awful lot of inchworms that liked them too, so it kept us busy thumping them off the berries, our buckets, and even our clothes. We were actually afraid of them.

Soon we'd have all the prettiest, big berries picked from that one spot and hurry off to another. Someone a little distance away would discover a big cache and yell out how nice they were over there so we'd all go sailing off over there and scramble around each other to see who could get the most and best.

As soon as we'd exhausted that supply we'd move on to some new territory. During all the moving around we were sure to encounter a snake of some sort so the process would come to a standstill till we got rid of him. From then on, we spent as much time looking for snakes as we did looking for berries.

The sun was awfully hot and no breeze could get to the congested, vine-infested areas where we were so it wasn't long till we were completely disenchanted with that job. As each one started a new complaint, we'd get more and more convinced that we had "a plenty of berries" for that trip. Anyway, we didn't want the "chiggers" to get too strong a hold on our bodies before we had a chance to wash them off. These little microscopic critters were very red bugs that crept onto your body via your clothes and dug right into your skin. They created a terrible itch which ultimately, after much scratching, turned into an infectious sore.

As we headed home, we'd canvass the vines we had passed up before and pick those few tiny berries to put in our not-so-full pails. Our mother was glad for us to return safe and sound, all but a few scratches in varying degrees. We'd shuck off all that extra garb, hang it on the garden fence hoping the hot sun would "de-chigger" them, get ourselves a pan of water and plenty of soap and start scrubbing. Sometimes we'd bathe again in alcohol or camphor hoping to kill the little red bugs.

A few of us seemed immune to them but some of us would get "et up" with them. We'd scratch the little devils, which were always worse around your navel, till we made full-fledged sores, then we'd doctor them with salty grease or anything else we'd heard of including kerosene.

Didn't seem like the whole thing was worth it but in a few days, we'd see some more ripened berries at which time we'd armor ourselves and go through the same procedures again.

The Bedbug Era

That old saying, "Good night, sleep tight, and don't let the bedbugs bite" was not just an old saying, it was purely concern for your neighbor's well being. Just like the plague of Japanese beetles or an onslaught of ants or Army worms, the bed bugs came and stayed a long time.

Due to the fact that there were few or no insecticides, these carnivorous little mischievous bugs were awfully hard to get rid of. Nobody knew for sure where they came from, but it was thought the pigeons had spread them all around. Since all the houses were made of wood boards, it was easy for them to crawl around and hide in the cracks between the boards.

All of the neighbors were reluctant to admit that they had any, but every spring when the weather got warm, they'd put those old wooden beds outside; sun the "straw ticks" (a large mattress-like cover for the bedsprings that was filled with straw), featherbeds, and pillows; hang all the quilts out on the clothes line or garden fences; and scrub down the walls.

We heated water and poured all over those beds, including the slats and side-rails, trying to kill the eggs of the bugs. The rooms sure did smell good when we put them all back together. Often we'd burn the old straw ticks and make brand new ones. It took a while to crumble up those new straws in the covers so that they didn't make a lot of noise and feel real rough when you moved around on them. The poor old featherbeds didn't get replaced often, if at all. Their covers were awfully spotted looking where we'd killed the bedbugs all over the corners. Periodically, we'd make new covers for them.

These plagued bugs would stay hidden during the day, but as soon as it got real dark and the lights were out they'd start scratching around, hunting human food. If one ever touched you, you couldn't sleep for hours. Every time the cover or anything touched you, you'd smack at it assuming it was a bedbug. Some nights, you'd even get

55

up, light a match, and look to see if you could find them. Sure enough, there would sometimes be several that you could spot and kill, any way you could, including smashing them on the bedcovers.

I don't recall anyone's having an infection caused by their bites, but there were a lot of sleepless nights with bags under your eyes that could have been accredited to them.

At intervals, our neighbors would come up with a sure way to get "shed" of them. One old farmer would announce that snuff would "run 'em off," another would come forth with the discovery that turpentine or sulfur put on the bed corners and locks would sure "kill 'em out." Someone else had got rid of them with stock dip. Those last two would scatter the usual bed occupants to the degree that the bedbugs would probably starve to death. Then everyone would declare war on the pigeons, thinking if you killed them all out that the bedbugs would be cornered. Sometimes, our parents even accused us of bringing them in from the neighbor's houses. Especially if they were suspected of not trying to get rid of theirs.

It took forever to make up a bed 'cause you had to look in every nook and cranny to see if you could find any bugs. It was especially disillusioning to change the pillowcases and bed sheets one day and then mess them up that night killing the bedbugs on them. Clean bed linens, or not, we never passed up an opportunity to kill one.

I don't know when they finally disappeared. I guess it was so gradual that it was hard to tell, but I suspect the invention of some pesticide can be credited with their demise.

One of our associates, who had gone to Cuba, said that place was eaten up with bedbugs, so maybe they preferred them and moved South; where it stays warm all year and they could feast on humans, non-stop and get fat, like their counterparts, the ticks.

The Family Reunion

On our family holidays mental calendar there were six days that were sacred and were not to be desecrated. They were Easter, Mothers' Day, the second Sunday in June, 4th of July, Thanksgiving, and Christmas. This second Sunday in June, which was in a lot of ways the most important, happened to be the day all of my Mother's sisters and brothers and their hundreds of descendants gathered for their annual family reunion.

No excuse was good enough not to attend. If you could move and breathe you went. If a close friend or relative died a few days previously you hurried to get them buried and proceeded with plans for the reunion. And another thing, if you weren't there those attending had a tendency to talk about you, and the remarks weren't always complimentary.

When you arrived at the designated place one of the first things on the agenda, after unloading your food and eating utensils, was to march by the elder honorees, who were either sitting in a circle or lined up in two lines, with women on one side and the men on the other. Here you received all those unwanted hugs and learned how much you had grown and how pretty you were getting. All of this was accompanied by our Mother's reporting on all our accomplishments like winning our school's spelling bee and singing in the Christmas program.

Being as how this was a traditional holiday, a special table had been built out of granite in each family member's yard. There were benches also made out of granite for us all to sit on, plus we usually carried a few chairs of our own to make sure we had a seat.

We always enjoyed going to the others' houses and seeing what they had done since the last meeting at their house. Everyone scattered out and looked at everything everywhere. Meanwhile, there was always some joker who'd reach out to shake hands with you with one of those buzzers in his hand. This, of course, made you jump or squeal, much to his delight. Then he'd go a little farther and meet up with another unsuspecting victim. He did this every year but we always tried to act surprised.

The very worst and most inefficient situation was the toilet problems. With about half of the attendants being small children you could never get in the toilet, which was of course on the outside. You'd wait around outside the toilet door for what seemed like hours, and even though you thought yours was an emergency, you'd notice a smaller kid standing first on one foot and then the other, or with his legs crossed, and you knew his problem took precedent over yours. So we'd amble off behind another building, like the men did, and relieve ourselves, hoping no one would walk up on us with the same thing in mind.

There was never a greater display of food than here. Every adult person brought at least three dishes each with iced tea, bread, and dessert. It was hard to decide where to start selecting food. The best way to tell where the good stuff was really found was to watch one of the "fatties" - they could spot the quality food by instinct, so often we'd just follow them around. Along with this abundance of rich food came the flies and ants - about 100 per person. We'd eat awhile and bat the gnats and flies. When we'd put our tea down to free up one hand someone would often mistakenly pick up our glass. If we turned our head to talk to someone the flies would descend on our most cherished food, but being used to them, we'd just knock them off and proceed as if nothing had happened. We always ate ourselves sick anyway.

The weather at this time of year was always hot, so the tea consumption was incredible . There were no Cokes, nor any other beverage except a little lemonade for those peculiar people who didn't like iced tea.

The tea was no ordinary tea; mostly it was "Tetley" and when you had already sweetened it while it was hot, you added a little extra sugar just in case the sweetness got weaker later. Often we'd bring a few sprigs of mint to make it even better. The ice didn't last very long because of the extreme heat but we'd "grabble" in it and add some to our tea glass as long as it lasted.

When the gluttonous eating finally came to a halt we'd saunter around to find someone our age and stand around and glance timidly at each other, hoping the other fellar would say or do something friendly. Occasionally someone would bring a ball along and a big gang of us would occupy ourselves with that or a good game of "hide-'n-seek." Top priority activity was to check out the wild plum bushes, if there were any, for ripening plums, even if poison oak was all around them.

One of my aunts who also had a big family, raised a bunch of musicians. They owned and could play almost every instrument known to us at that time. They were a real talented bunch and we were all very pleased for them all to get tuned up and render a few numbers. Sometimes they'd even sing to go with it, and if we knew the song we'd sing along with them.

These large and important gatherings rotated from house to house, and there were special things at each place that we enjoyed; however, as the population explosion continued the crowds got bigger and bigger, and we eventually had to move our gathering place to a centrally located church. Here the toilet facilities! were a little better; they even had two separate buildings for girls and boys. Disappointingly, though, they didn't have a Sears, Roebuck catalogue.   They just had plain newspapers.

The goodbyes lasted about as long as the reunions. We kids had been up for the longest and were sleepy and tired, and about half sick from eating too much. We were more than ready to go home, but our Mother had to tell each and every person how good it was to see them and to come see us, knowing full well we wouldn't see most of them again till the next second Sunday in June.

When It Snowed

Other than Christmas and Easter, the snows were by far the most exciting things in our young lives. The ecstatic sounds that echoed through our house when our dad, who was the first one up, announced it had snowed, could be heard far and near. As cold as our floors were, we'd bail out of bed in our bare feet and run to every window and door to look out and make sure we weren't dreaming. We'd bang on each other, hop up and down, maybe even hug each other and start making plans for the day.

Dad was busy scrambling around getting at least two fires started along with one in the cook stove, while we made a bee-line for our assigned dresser drawers to find our most appropriate warm clothes so we could get outside. Each one of us was wild with anticipation about making a snowman, or a snowball battle, or sliding down our steep hill in the pasture and finding some good clean snow for some snow ice cream.

As soon as we were dressed while breakfast was being prepared, we'd sneak out the doors and yank off some icicles from anything we could reach and come back inside with them dripping all over the house. With our hands as cold as they could get, we'd sneak around and put them down someone's collar to hear them squeal. Anyway, with snow outside, breakfast was strictly secondary.

We ate as fast as our Dad would let us and got out in that cold wet mess and started slipping and sliding and pulling each other down. The most fun, 'cause it was dangerous, was sliding down our steep hill toward the branch. There was no stopping once we got started, so turning our improvised sled over was the way we got off. The long hard walk back up the hill was awfully tiring, but we'd hack it for a few more rides. It didn't take very long for us all to be completely exhausted and frozen stiff then we'd trudge or slide back to the doorsteps, where we'd often have to crawl up. Some of us have lasting reminders of falling on our bottoms down the steps. 'Twas very injurious to our spines.

As soon as we'd get on the porches, we'd start de-robing and flinging soggy wet clothes all over the place. Next, we'd have to remove the soaked shoes and socks. We'd all make a beeline to get in front of one of the fires. We'd shove each other out of the way and turn from front to back, trying to warm up. Our legs would turn reddish, purple, checkered after standing there for so long.

When our mother announced that we'd have to stay inside, we'd all whine and moan in unison and plead to her, reminding her that there might not be another snow this whole year or next year.

Finding clean, dry replacement clothes was a real challenge. We'd even get our sister's and brother's socks or underwear, or whatever else we needed to get warmed up.

In order to get us all calmed down, our mother would let a bigger kid get some good clean snow to make ice cream. The bigger kid had specific instructions to only get snow where the hounds and chickens had not been. Us younger ones wouldn't have been so particular. She'd use all of our morning milk and make a whole dish pan full of snow cream. This was the fastest concoction you could whip up. All it took was milk, sugar, vanilla flavoring, and snow. It had to be eaten instantly or it was all watery and tasteless. Of course, it was all gone instantly at our house; as fast as it could be dished out.

This treat only lasted a few minutes and then we were back to our original plans for making a snowman. We had to stay inside a while and be noisy and disagreeable in order for our mother to consent for us to play outside again. Sure enough, after a while, she'd "give in" and out we went, wearing everything in the house that was dry.

Sometimes the snow didn't pack so good, but we'd pat and roll and bang around on it till we had a resemblance of a snowman, then we'd sneak inside and find buttons and an old hat or coat to put the finishing touches on.

Usually we could find some sticks or coal pieces for eyes, buttons, and cigars. Sometimes our big evil brothers would come out and snatch his coat off 'cause it belonged to them. They didn't care how cold the poor snowman got.

We wouldn't be outside for long before a snowball fight erupted. What started out as fun, usually turned into real combat, bawling and all. We'd throw or fling snow at each other for revenge until our Dad came to the door and made us all come inside. Here we'd start that drying up process again.

With wet clothes draped all over the chairs, door knobs, tables, and on top of the doors, you couldn't touch anything that was dry. It was hard for us to visualize how "them kids up North" stood all that snow and dampness for the entire winter, as hard as it was for us to get through only one day!?!

Sunday Evenin' Singings

One of the most widely attended social functions in our locale was the "church singings." Under strong leadership, they were carried on all year long, From one church to another in the neighboring communities; even over into the surrounding counties. They were well attended and actually enjoyed by some.

Everyone considered himself a potential song-leader and went with those expectations. The transportation presented no more of a problem than anything else, if you had a car or could bum a ride you rode; otherwise, you walked. The admission was one of the best things about it all - free!

The probably self-appointed, leader in our area was not the best qualified man for the job. He had no personality, was not aggressive and downright back woodsy His main qualifications, being he had a car and was willing to go at all costs, plus he had "umpteen" sons, whom he desperately wanted to make singers out of.

They were long, lanky, dingy, country fellows who had terrible haircuts and little to no ability to perform. Their father had taught them the basic notes and they could read most of the words in the song books. This was a hand picked book with all the Country favorites, which were really gospel tunes, and were usually sung at a foot patting tempo as loud as you could holler.

The piano player was selected because he or she could add all kinds of extra jubilant notes before and after each stanza and play loud and fast. Whether or not they could really read music was not even considered. It you knew too much about music, you usually didn't attend these functions.

When the word was spread that "They're havin' a sangin' Sunday evenin'" at whatever church, everyone started making plans to go. Often, these included brushing up on hitting the high notes and singing loud so as to be in

63

good shape in case you were asked to lead a number or two.

As soon as several folks had arrived at the church, found a good front seat and A fan, or warmed by the heater, the leader would start looking around for prospects to lead the songs. When the program got underway, without fail, the leader would march all of his sons out with their Sunday finest on, including clean or new shoes, line 'em up and give 'em the downbeat. The eager piano player would hit those starting notes (always the same); father would beat the time with his big rough hands and the noise was underway. You hated to poke your fingers in your ears or pull your cap down over them to muffle the sound, but I know it would have sounded a lot better.

The sounds ranged from nasally, to high pitched, to guttural, to bellowing. No one but their immediate family enjoyed that segment, but it was always nice to get it over with. Then another being was summoned to lead the next song. Often there was a real outstanding alto, bass, or soprano that could belt out more volume than the rest of the crowd and of course, everyone turned around in their seat to see who they were, for they would surely be called upon to lead the next several songs.

Late comers or crying babies were completely ignored and the foot-patting was just a part of the service. The only reason these functions were held in the church was because it could seat a lot of people and no one had to clean up before nor afterward. The program was certainly not a worshipful one nor had the audience come for that purpose. It was just another community get-together where a lot of people had the opportunity to be seen and heard and let the rest of the world hear how good they could sing.

There were timid people who would hardly utter a word when you came in contact with them outside those doors, but at singings, when called upon, they make haste getting to the starting spot, near the piano with a song all picked out, yell out the page number, and without any hesitation, belt out one of those old familiar

64

tunes. Then they'd march right back to their seats with their heads tucked like always, quiet as a mouse.

Very few people, if any, refused to go up and lead a song. Only occasionally someone who could not possibly carry a tune and who recognized that fact would fidget around in his seat, fumble with his songbook, and come out with, I ain't no sanger." Guess all the others figured they couldn't do any worse than their predecessors.

When everyone's throats got sore and they'd stood all they could of listening to not too talented newcomers making their debuts and the not too impressive old timers exerting themselves, the crowd would slowly disband and start trying! to find a volunteer church to host the next great event.

The Shaving Ritual

Since we lived out in the "boonies" and we mostly worked in the fields and woods, my Dad and brothers didn't see any need to shave every day, so they didn't. Two or three times a week, in most cases, was the limit. With all the fan fare and griping that preceded the dreaded chore, we were very glad they didn't.

This was the era when you shaved with a straight razor. This item looked like A weapon or a butcher's knife. We were terribly afraid when we saw our Dad's face bleed so profusely after a good slicing from them.

The forerunner for the ritual was "strapping" the razor. For this there was a 2 ½ inch wide leather band that was kept hanging on the back porch. It was never moved except when it was in use by the authority. Actually it was a dual purpose "strap." Along with being a sharpener for the razors, it also served as a whipping apparatus for the big "young'uns" who had misbehaved. At any rate and for all purposes, we did not touch it nor enjoy seeing it as it hung there.

With the razor all sharpened up and tested by cutting a single strand of hair, the rest of the operation got under way. The same face cloth had to be used, the same washbasin, the same shaving brush and cup, the same mirror, and the same spot. No matter how close these were to my Dad, he could never find them and his voice would ring throughout the house with, "Who's had my shaving brush?"

As soon as he'd been waited on hand and face, he'd settle down with some hot water and a steaming cloth held over his face to soften the beard. This took several minutes. With the right amount of silence and stillness, he'd proceed to lather up his face. We loved that part, he looked like "Father Time." We thought that was a most peculiar look and always watched that part.

Then he'd gingerly pick up the super sharp razor and start stretching his mouth from one side to the other.

66

With the other hand, he'd pull the skin tight and start scraping the lather and whiskers off. All went well for a few minutes, and then when he got to the small areas he'd nip a little flesh and it would start bleeding. We all knew when this happened, he'd blurt out all the slang combinations he knew, in a real loud bellow. Someone would rush to the rescue with a little bit of paper napkin or tissue paper saved for just that purpose. With several other "nicked" places on his face, and the job almost finished, he'd often get disgusted and yell for one of my older brothers to come finish the job. I'm sure they dreaded that 'cause his temperament wasn't too good by that time.

He'd dictate every move and really growl when he thought they weren't doing it right. Somehow, they'd get through it and plaster his face with all those bits of paper, which he wore a half a day. Some of us would clean up behind them, everything being put back in its right place till the next production.

We were all glad for our Dad to get shaved at the local barber shop which was in the back of what used to be our Dad's General Merchandise Store. He looked a lot cleaner without all those little paper plasters all over his face and it saved us all a lot of anxiety, including him.

Getting Ready For Christmas

We looked forward to Christmas from one year to the next. Even getting ready for it was exciting. Since there was very little money and very few available decorations, we had to make a lot of plans and use even more ingenuity.

First on the agenda was finding the Christmas tree! Three or four of us would get the rifle and a few cartridges, an axe, put on a heavy wrap and cap and gloves, if we could find any, and head out in search of the perfect tree. Ours was always cedar, because our parents had always used cedar, and they grew in abundance in our area. That is, until we thinned them out trying to find the right one for our house every year.

We'd walk awhile, shoot at the birds or rabbits, or whatever was alive, other than ourselves and the cows. Sometimes we'd kill something if it were too slow to move away, but mostly we just shot. Then we'd proceed till we saw a cedar bush. We'd cut this one down in case we didn't find a better one. If and when we found another we'd also cut that one down and continue our search. This was strictly our kind of fun, so we'd stay out in the woods till the sun was getting low or the weather started getting cooler, then we'd choose between the trees and either carry or drag it as we headed for home.

Finding the old decorations to trim the tree took a while, 'cause they got moved around from one closet to another during the year. Closet space was at a premium, since there was only one per room, except in the boys' room. They had two. When winter came and all the spare covers were in use on the beds, there was a lot of storage space, so we always rearranged things.

The poor ole limp roping made of a crepe paper substance sure showed wear and a lot of it had to be sewed back together to wrap around the tree. Just because a glass ball was broken didn't mean we discarded it; we hung it up right amongst the good ones and paid no further attention to it. We never did have

68

popcorn strings for our tree, we probably ate up all the popcorn! The old tinsel sticks were tarnished and could hardly be seen. T'was a great improvement when they made shredded strips of tinsel.

If we found a cute celluloid toy that wasn't heavy, we'd hang it on the tree. By today' standards, it wasn't much of a Christmas tree, but back then we thought it was beautiful. Next on the agenda was the search for holly and mistletoe. The latter was always away up in a tall tree, where you couldn't possibly get to it, so we'd throw rocks or shoot at it till some little branches fell out. We thought we had to have it, but after we got it we sure didn't make much use of it. We did tack a sprig over the door, but we were much too bashful to kiss anyone standing under it.

The holly was wild and grew out in the woods, but never in abundance. We'd look and look before we finally found an old scraggly tree. Being as determined as we were, we managed to get a few limbs along with all kinds of scratches and bruises. I think the only advantage of having holly was the fact that it was dark greenish with a scant sprinkling of reddish berries that half-way brightened things up, and, anyway, it was a cherished tradition plus it didn't cost us a cent.

As soon as we got home we'd start immediately rearranging the vases and pictures, and ceramic figurines to find just the right spot for the holly. Sometimes we'd even move the crocheted dresser scarves to get that festive look. The fireplaces had to have a fresh coat of "whitewash" that really brightened up the rooms. We also washed and starched the window curtains to make the rooms look fresh and nice.

With the house all decorated to the hilt our Mother got us busy picking out pecans and grating coconut for some of those 8 to 10 Christmas cakes and ambrosia. We had every kind of cake there was and some that didn't have a "kind;" she kinda combined recipes and whipped up some original ones.

69

We even had homemade candies. I'll always remember that yummy divinity and buttermilk candy that was so tasty. Grating the coconuts (and knuckles) was the hardest job. It was impossible to keep from grating your fingers; if there hadn't been so many kids standing around asking for the little "nubs" you simply couldn't grate, there would have been hands full of sore fingers.

As soon as all the cooking was done or under way, we'd start piling wood on the porch and kitchen wood box, we'd also round up some kindling, as our only source of heat was the fireplaces and the kitchen stove. At this point we were ready for ole Santa Claus, except for writing messages to him on the bottoms of our assorted Christmas boxes that we set out (instead of hanging up stockings), one big room was completely filled up with boxes on Christmas Eve in hope that ole Santa would have enough goodies to put something in all of them. He always did.

When The Radio Got Turned On

Radios away back when I was a kid were a sacred piece of machinery. "No one, but no one" dared to try to operate it but the head of the house or his designated assistant. The technology of switching the knob on and off was not child's play. I think that I'm safe in saying that no one under 30 was allowed to even move it. We usually dusted around it or on top of it lightly.

It was turned on in the early morning, mostly to find out if the world had come to an end or if any other such catastrophic events had happened. Foreign affairs weren't particularly interesting since we didn't know which continent what country was in anyway, so very little emphasis was placed on it. With his ear glued to the speaker part, my Dad listened intently for a few minutes, then switched "her" off so as to not run the batteries down.

At about lunch time, we'd listen to a newscast plus they had some wonderful live country music. This also included Western songs, tear jerking ballads, and just plain down-home instrumental numbers. At any rate, it was all too good to miss so we sat or stood at attention and no one spoke or moved around till it was time to turn the radio off once more. Around this time of day on a nearby station, two of my older sisters were featured on a program that advertised flour.

Their talents were playing the fiddle and guitar and singing. At our house, all operations came to a halt so we could listen to each and every word along with all the music. In keeping with the times, we kept busy writing down lyrics and learning the tunes to all new songs we heard from any source. Often the words and tunes would vary slightly from the original but back then few people noticed 'cause when they themselves picked up bits and pieces of a new song, they were also different. It was hard to know what the real words were and if the tune really went up or down at a certain point. It didn't really matter for most of us 'cause the only place most of them

71

got sung was in the fields or pastures and the ole mules sure didn't know the difference.

All the mothers or older women and some younger women, near and far, had to listen to that world renown soap opera, "Ma Perkins." "Ma Perkins" captivated the whole society and was everyone's role model, if not idol. This program was discussed with the same interest as that of a member of your family and was not "fiction" to most people, it was "real life" stuff that had to be reckoned with. Nobody dared to say an unkind word about "Ma Perkins." This must have been the originator of the modern radio and T.V. Soaps.

Another really unusual program that one of my older brothers liked and wouldn't miss, featured a guy picking a guitar and singing little fragments of news items that he had rhymed and set to his own music. After each verse he'd sing,"I don't reckon that'll happen again in months 'n months" and repeat it again. Sometimes it was funny and clever and at other times it just occupied the space, like all other programs.

It was hard to tell if "Lum and Abner" (with their telephone answer of "Jot 'em Down Store, Lum Edwards speaking") was better than "Amos n' Andy" or vice versa; we'd catch ourselves tattling (to the radio) on the misbehaving pranksters and reprimanding of the evil-doers, or telling "Mama and Sapphire" to shut up. We were so involved in their situations and helping them solve their problems, we couldn't believe it when the program was over. We'd just as soon have them stay on 24 hrs. a day.

There were wrestling and boxing matches carried on a regular basis, but unless our mother was away from home we didn't get to hear them. She also didn't care for baseball. Our dad would have listened but he just didn't have time for all the good stuff the radio had to offer.

Now Saturdays were looked forward to with great anticipation because of the high standard programs that we could get on the radio (weather permitting), Quite often the batteries were so weak or the static was so bad that we could hardly tell what we had picked up, but the knob stayed on the same station. At lunchtime, fresh out of Atlanta, we could pick up "Harpo Kidwell and the Blue Sky Boys" along with a few other "pickers and singers," but the very best and ultimate in good entertainment came on at night. Everyone hurried around, got his Saturday bath early, ate, and got his chair positioned and could hardly wait for the big events to get underway.

Almost always we'd pick up the Grand Ole Opry with all those fabulous advertisements. Those featured favorite entertainers like Uncle Dave Macon and his son Doris, Bill Monroe and the Blue Grass Boys, Minnie Pearle, Roy Acuff, etc., kept us spellbound. We were so addicted to those programs we even thought we had to use the products they advertised.

It was a long shot, but occasionally we could get the "Louisiana Hay Ride" and the "Chicago Barn Dance." This was really stepping in high cotton. We remembered every performer, every song, and every instrument they played. All this was information that we could relay to the poor people who hadn't been able to hear the program, or we just exchanged opinions about how "good" each was with our friends. We never talked about how bad or corny they were because we didn't know they came any better.

As soon as the programs were over (midnight in some instances), we'd move away from the radio trying to sing some different number we'd heard and could hardly wait till the next Saturday night to see if we could pick up the rest of the tune to a new song.

On Sunday mornings, our dad would fine-tune the treasured entertainment box to some gospel singers. It seemed like the whole world was into gospel singing. They went on forever with groups from all the neighboring states participating. When they finally let up the "Hell Fire and Damnation" preachers got underway. Those boys were really wound up tight. They'd rant and rave till their time slots ran out. The mild mannered preachers were few and far between, guess the sponsors thought you couldn't hear it if you weren't yelled at.

73

Eventually, the batteries or not-so-good radio went on the blink. When a new set of batteries was installed, if that was the problem, you could hear that radio all the way out in the yard. We were thrilled over that installation; you would have thought it was Christmas. Now we could really tell what the words to some of those songs were and hear every word "Ma Perkins" said, plus we got even more involved in those "Lum and Abner" and "Amos 'n Andy" series.

The Square Dances

In the middle of winter, when the worst weather and the doldrums had set in, beginning their long dreaded reign, the happiest words we could ever hope to hear were those announcing a square dance. "Saddy Night." Our square dances were held in private homes and kinda by invitation so as to keep the worst drunkards and complete strangers away. That kind of ensured an orderly or decent affair.

There weren't many parents who would consent to hosting them, as the trouble of moving all of the furniture out of a room and probably hallway turned out to be a headache; not to mention cleaning up the mud, chewing gum wrappers, cigar/cigarette butts and whiskey jars or cans on the outside after the dance since the yards were all dirt, in the event of bad weather, many cars mired up and made deep ruts across the yard and nearby fields. Some of them even got stuck.

The rooms without fireplaces were picked so the music makers and dancers wouldn't get too hot or get too close to the fire and scorch their clothes. The music makers were carefully selected (only those who would or could come and play were considered). A couple of our older sisters were asked to play sometimes. They liked the money but despised some of the crowds and being out so late (sometimes till 12:00). One of our brothers always played. He put all he had in to his guitar picking, with volume making up for quality. He'd pat his foot and sway to the tunes of "Down Yonder," "Little Lisa Jane," "Under the Double Eagle," etc. He was the main reason that I was allowed to go. My mom would give her okay, we'd get dressed and away we went! One of my older brothers was my favorite dance partner; we would deviate from the normal format and giggle and show off all we pleased. Actually, he was a good dancer, but everyone was apprehensive about asking someone to dance, so when things got dull we'd just dance together. It was most embarrassing for the guys to be rejected when they finally worked up sufficient courage to ask a girl to dance.

The girls' criteria for accepting a dance partner was whether or not he'd been drinking in the long run, everyone danced with everyone else on the dance floor, with all the "do, si, do-ing," "gathering up four," etc. Some of the really ugly guys and girls had a hard time finding someone to dance with them. The unescorted girls and boys without dates stood around and observed the prospects before launching out in search of a partner.

As soon as the music makers were in place and the "caller" found a good spot, things would get into full swing. The rafters would sway a little along with the floors. The regular dancers would come forward and ring up and start moving around with a lot of gusto, swinging and stomping, and sweating trying to hear what the "caller" was saying. A lot of older folks were seated around the wall some would sing or clap, or pat their feet to the music. It was the perfect time to unwind and be merry.

There was always an intermission or two to let the musicians (?) smoke a cigarette or go to the toilet and also to let the dancers wipe sweat and unwind and start hunting a partner for the next session. A lot of bashful glances were exchanged, and sometimes a timid conversation developed. Several marriages came out of some of these encounters, since that was one of the few places to meet anybody except at church.

Money, even coins, was very scarce, and a lot of guys would make a point of leaving the dance early so as not to be embarrassed by not putting something in the hat for the musicians when the dance was over. The pay was puny in most cases, but the pleasure derived from being important enough to be asked to play more than compensated for it.

Our mother did not really approve of those dances, so she never let us have one at our house, and I'm sure she wouldn't have agreed to her children playing for them if there had been any other way to make a buck.

76

The Beloved Tacky Parties

I can't imagine why a "tacky party" would be so appealing to us unless, like at Halloween we felt appropriate for the occasion. The very best most of us looked was tacky, but we didn't realize it at the time, so we just proceeded with our plans, "full speed ahead."

Our mother would let us have some of those parties. As soon as the idea received full backing, we'd get busy and ring-up (on our old crank style telephone) everyone we wanted to come. Most of the time you'd only have to ring two or three people. Everyone eavesdropped on all the telephone conversations, so the word got around real fast. When you rang a number, everyone's phone would ring, so everyone ran to listen in on all the conversation. You could hardly hear the person you had called for all the clicks and hanging up noises of everyone else. At any rate, you wound up with more guests than you really wanted to come, due to that haphazard telephone system.

It took a lot of preparing to get yourself ready for one of those parties, 'cause You wanted to have on the tackiest outfit of anyone, plus you had to plan all the games and make arrangements for the refreshments (which were not the real reason anyone would come).

We put more emphasis on how we dressed than all the other considerations put together. We'd borrow our Dad's or Mom's clothes 'cause they were too big (back then, big was not stylish). Often we'd wear the shirt or blouse backward or inside out put the hats or caps on sideways or backwards, wear big shoes on the wrong feet, put on one sock of one color and one sock of another on the other foot and wear extra long or short skirts or dresses. The guys would wear their pants that were too short or roll one leg up and leave the other down, accompanied by two or three shirts. All of this would be topped off with assorted brooches, neckties, necklaces, earrings, bracelets, and scarves draped in every direction.

In order to match the garb, we had to style the hair and wear messy makeup accordingly. The games were antiquated and over-used because of their simplicity and lack of expense. We'd rig up the semblance of a donkey and make a batch of tails with which we'd play "pin the tail on the donkey." With the chosen one blindfolded, we either turned the picture upside down or turned the "pinner" around a few times to confuse him and head him out in the wrong direction. This game was always fun to us. Another favorite was "cross-questions and crooked answers." We did wonders with this and even though the objective was to give your response without laughing, no one ever did. The questions were so ridiculous like "What time did you leave?", and the absurd reply would be, "We ate it all up with our crackers." The longer we played this game the funnier It got A lot of the time we'd play "pass the thimble" or "musical chairs" or "what's your trade?", or have a blindfolded person in the middle of a circle guess who they were standing in front of.

When we tired of all those games, we'd sing the ole routine, "Row, row, row your boat" or "Down by the Old Millstream" or "Are you sleeping?" We took time in between games to whisper to each other and giggle and try to sneak off to go to the toilet. You would have died rather than let any of the fellars know you ever went to the toilet. They, themselves, would wander off out of the room and disappear for a few minutes without any fanfare and we hardly even noticed. After all this carrying-on, it was about "party over time," so we'd line up and eat refreshments and decide who was the tackiest.

The refreshments were very ordinary homemade cookies or cake and punch or lemonade. As I reiterated before, the refreshments were no main reason to come, and, of course, there were no prizes for the tackiest just the satisfaction of winning.

When the seasons were dull and the hardest work on the farm was over, we'd often resort to another "tacky party," just to have somewhere to go at night.

The Box Suppers

When a special need for funds for the church or school came up, the idea of a box supper was always mentioned as one of the pet projects.

Boxes were not really eaten as the name implies. Food was prepared and auctioned off in boxes as a supper for two. Whoever prepared the food plus whoever placed the highest bid for the box were the two.

These benefits were usually held at the school house in the community and were announced in the usual manner by the "eavesdropper" telephone system and the local country store where most of the news was dispatched.

This was a good place for a guy to come in contact with the girl of his dreams that he wouldn't dare just up and ask for a date or for those bashful couples who already had a claim on each other, but didn't get together often. The guys had to save up their money and make sure they made the highest bid on those girls' boxes so they could have the pleasure of eating and talking with her.

The general procedure for fixing-up a box was to prepare meat with bread, a salad, pickles, sandwiches, and a dessert for two people and display it as nice as they could in a "beribboned" box that favored a gift package. The boxes were often attractive even though they had previously contained everything from shoes to motor oil.

The fellows came as early as possible so as to get a good look at the girls who brought each box. They weren't taking any chances on bidding on a pretty box with an ugly or stupid girl for a bonus. Rumors were that some of the families weren't too clean with their cooking or were not very good cooks. One family even kept cats in their house and you sure didn't want to eat food from that source.

I'm sure the girls had reservations about having their boxes bought by some obnoxious, bad looking guy and having to eat its contents with that creep. She'd most likely be kidded 'til dooms day about that "new boyfriend". On the other hand, her box might get very few bids and that would certainly be embarrassing.

With all these drawbacks, it's a wonder the "box suppers" were successful at all but with everyone in the community being "civic minded" and closely monitored for their presence at such affairs, there was no easy way out. You just fixed up a box, saved up your money and went. These were kind of a "hey day" for the bachelors in the neighborhood. They usually had the money and if they had admired a certain girl who now had a regular boyfriend, it was his chance to try to break them up by making the highest bid on her box and sharing it with her. For this occasion, he'd put on his best starched white shirt with rolled-up long sleeves, stiffly starched pants, a pair of good socks with no holes in the heels, a fresh white handkerchief and he was all ready for some excitement.

Sometimes, he'd run the bids up as high as $3-$5 a box or come up with "more than one box to have to eat!!!" A real problem???

The highest bidder and the preparer often took their boxes and opened them up on the outside to eat the food. The fellow felt obligated to compliment the food no matter how bad or soggy or scrambled together it was and of course, the embarrassed girl would often reply with something like, "I appreciate your buying my box," or "I'm glad you like fried chicken and caramel cake, I cooked it myself."

There was talk that the people who came to clean up the next day said a good half of the food had been thrown away. It would have been funny to see how that was handled. Could have been a box was "accidently" turned over or while the girl looked off the fellar sneaked some food and dropped it behind him. A few times the girls were lucky enough to be escorted home by their box buyers and asked for a date on another occasion.

80

A Hunting We Did Go

One coolish fall afternoon an old lost hound dog came up to our house. He had that "I'm lost and haven't had a bite to eat in two days" look; so being kind-hearted dog lovers, we threw him some old bread scraps which he woofed down instantly, and thereafter made himself completely at home. Having failed in our efforts to run him off, we entertained the thought of perhaps taking him on a possum hunt.

This idea got bigger and better as the day progressed, so we launched off to the store to see if we could drum up some interest from some other sources. Several of our friends and their friends sounded interested, and as luck would have it, one of them even had a caged possum; another could use his dad's ole truck, so the hunt was on.

Close to dark we rounded up an old lantern, untied the dog, and met the other hunters at the specified place (a big old oak tree by the cemetery). The group was kinda young, 12-16, with about nine kids in the crowd, mostly giggly girls. The feller with the truck was young too, but you didn't have to have a driver's license back then.

Now, the special requirements for possum hunting were a pocket full of peanuts, some shoes, and a jacket - so everyone was all set. As soon as we'd all placed ourselves on the truck, along with the dog and the possum, we took off over an open field toward a wooded area.

Just this side of a weeded-over ditch, we unloaded, lit up the lantern, and untied the dog. We then hastened to uncage the possum, stomped our feet so he would run, and then took off behind him in hot pursuit. So hot, in fact, about half of us stepped or fell into the ditch, which had concealed water in it. That made things a little cooler than we had expected, along with slowing us down.

By this time it was really dark and everyone was hovering close to the lantern, which didn't provide much

81

more light than a match. In fact, the person with the lantern was the only one who could see where to step. We couldn't move fast for untangling the briers and pushing the bushes out of our faces. Our ole dog messed around and lost sight of the possum and evidently didn't know what he was supposed to do or was scared, so he just hung around the lantern.

With our possum gone, our feet wet, the ole disinterested dog under our feet, and unable to see where we were going, we just ate up the peanuts and giggled and told tacky jokes and stumbled back toward the truck. We did manage to leave the dog there, and the truck didn't break down, so from there things went pretty smooth till we were all dropped off at our respective places of abode.

Candy Pulling

"Pull Candy" was really what we called taffy only we really pulled it by hand and a lot of the time ours was made out of sorghum syrup.

There were private family candy pullings and then there were a few brave souls who invited friends to come to their houses to make candy. Those who had been host before knew what a mess it involved and almost never made the same mistake twice.

The younger participants couldn't have cared less about the boiled over or spattered sweet, sweet mess; not to mention all of the scorched utensils and dirty pans and dishes (and floors) there were to clean up afterwards. It was just plain fun to them and good eating once you got a batch cooked up at the right proportions.

First off, you had to have a large heavy cook pan, a long-handled spoon, a lot of sorghum syrup and butter, and a pinch of soda. As soon as you got the stove all fixed up to the right temperature, you set the large pan of syrup on the right eyes and started stirring. There were no adjustable knobs for cooling or heating, so you just stood there and burned up as the temperature soared and the syrup boiled. You were lucky if it didn't pop out and burn you on your arms or face and if it didn't boil over. In the latter case, you'd fumble around trying to find a not so sticky spot to hold to and hope the lifting pad was thick enough to allow you to move the pan and try to get it off the main heat.

As soon as things cooled off a little, you'd proceed to cook the stuff till it made a soft ball in cold water or spun from the spoon when lifted away up over the pan. Most of the time, it was hit and miss, but usually it was all right if you could pull it long enough.

As soon as it was decided to be of the right consistency to pull, we'd start buttering our hands. After much stirring to cool it, we'd take out a small amount of the syrup "goop" and wallow it from one hand to the other to further cool it. After a while, we'd start stretching it with both hands. If it were still hot we'd make fast motions, and sometimes even drop it on the floor. Then we'd snatch it up real fast, look for trash or dirt, which we'd remove and continue on with the pulling process. By this time we'd need someone to help us. They would add their little wad to ours and we'd pull it back and forth till it was real light colored and hard to pull. By that time it was "ready," so we'd lay it on a buttered dish and wait for it to get cool and ready to cut up or break into pieces.

Then we'd start eating it immediately. If there were company involved, we'd start another batch and proceed in the same manner. You also had to be real careful not to let your hair get stuck up in it. We weren't too concerned about the sanitation of the thing, we just didn't want to lose a plug of hair where it would show the most. We often ate so much of the super sweet stuff we'd feel sick all night and not really want any more syrup candy for quite a while.

The Wash Hole

You just hadn't arrived if you didn't have a "wash hole." By definition, that's a dammed-up creek or branch (small stream of water). We had a good spot for one, but it was only a few feet from a very cold "spring" (water that bubbles up from a deep source) and in a shady place.

The tall banks on each side of the branch were perfect for the dam, and we had the work force, after recruiting a few interested neighbor kids. The whole project was undertaken after the cotton was chopped and the corn was weeded and fertilized and "laid by" (left to fend for itself).

On a sunny afternoon, the group assembled at our house with shovels and hoes and a wheelbarrow, at which time we ran or walked down a steep hill to the spring. About 120 feet downstream, we set up operations with digging and shoveling and hauling in the process of damming up the branch so the water would start backing up to where it'd be at least knee deep. One time we made one almost to our waists.

It was so hot handling all those tools we'd spend about as much time in the pond as out. Sometimes we'd bring a big watermelon and let it cool in the spring while we worked, but as soon as our mouths started watering, we'd go cut it up and eat it, get a cool drink of water from the gourd dipper that stayed at the spring, and go back to hauling more dirt. When we'd dig dirt from the outside of the banks, wiggle-tails would get in the little pond that accumulated there. We spent some of our time watching them wiggle around. The water snakes were bad to inhabit our wash holes, so we kept an ever watchful eye for them. If one was spotted, the alarm went off and everyone proceeded to throw rocks and sticks at the varmint till it went somewhere else.

This dammed up water had to have an outlet so's the cows and mules could have something to drink further down the branch, so we selected a competent person and put him or her in charge of the "run-around" - this also kept the water from running over the top and washing the dam away.

Sometimes this whole operation took more than one afternoon to build, so when everyone was thoroughly exhausted, we'd call a halt and try the ole swimming pond out. Back then there were very few "official" swim suits (if any) in our community, so we brought along some old clothes to go wading in, especially if there was mixed company and most of the time there was. The water was very cold and muddy, but in spite of it all, we'd dive in, hold our noses, and dunk our heads under, duck each other, splash, kick, flap, wade, and really cool off; a most rewarding treat for such a hard job.

One little feller came running down the hill when he heard all the merriment to join in the fun. He had just had his Saturday bath and was wearing some brand new overalls. He was so intent on joining the group he just yanked an old dress on over all his clothes and hopped in. As soon as we realized he had on his good clothes we got him out and showed him what a mess he'd made. This, of course, made him cry, 'cause he was quite young and had no idea the water would go through all his clothes and mess up his new overalls!

But if it rained very much at all, down went the dam and all the water. We couldn't wait to run down the hill after each rain to see if the wash hole was still there. If it were washed away and it looked like the rains were over, we'd get right on to building another one. After all, it was the only way we had to really cool off during the hot summer weather, plus it sufficed for a bath every now and then.

The Big Deep Gully

Soil erosion was a big problem in our locale, the kids thought it was a blessing, it created some good places to play and hide. What used to be little streams of ditches kept washing away till in some cases they were very deep gullies. Our cow pasture had one such gully and we believed it to be very mysterious, probably a hiding place for Trolls under a bridge over the road that led to another farmer's house.

Each time we walked across that bridge, we'd peep over into that deep crevice to see if we could see any boogers. A snake or any other varmint would be considered a booger. If our mother sent us into the pasture for any reason, we'd always go by and check out the deep gully first.

There were several little washed out trenches that led to the gully and we'd proceed carefully, holding onto each other down one of them to the lower-most part of the ravine to see if there were anything new down there. We never attempted these daring feats alone. There'd be at least two or three of us in case we needed help.

Occasionally, we'd find a spring lizard or snake. Either one would frighten us as we were expecting the worst. Someone in the group would capture a crawfish or pretend to have a lizard to try to put on one of us. We'd all squeal and run as fast as we could trying to keep out of reach till we found out it was a hoax. We'd continue walking down the branch looking for anything out of the ordinary. Sometimes, we'd happen up on some minnows and try to catch one. After hopelessly pursuing that for a while, we'd move on to something else.

Next stop could be to yank down a hanging vine for a new jump rope, or maybe we'd find an overhanging limb that we could swing across on or jump down from. Located in the lower and most shallow part of this gully was our "White Dirt Hole." Here was a good source for that stuff and it was considered quite valuable for painting up and around fireplaces when they weren't in use and some tree trunks or rocks.

It was a very smooth gray mud that we dug up and carried home in a big pail. When we needed it we'd mix water with it and smear it on and around the fireplace to cover the smoke discolored areas and make them white. Sometimes we'd smear some on our faces and arms. That made them feel very clean when we washed it off (could have been the beginning of face masks).

At one point close to the bridge where we had a barbed wire fence, there was a muscadine vine that completely crossed the gully. Seems all the pretty muscadines were hanging right over the middle of the ravine at the deepest part. When the time came for them to be ripe, we'd take a big pan and round up some volunteers then head for the hunting grounds (rather gullies).

One of us would shake the vines and about two or three would wobble down in a little ditch to the gully's bottom with our paws ready to pick up all we could get to. We'd gather all we could for this trip and go back in a few days to go through the same ritual. Nothing tasted any better to us than muscadine pie made from the hulls or juice which our mother often canned for winter.

At another lower part of the gully was some incredibly beautiful moss. This was needed to carpet our playhouse floors. It was hard to transfer, and often we'd scoop it up with our bare hands and pile it in our dress tails to carry it with us.

Still further down the gully, where the banks were not so steep, we'd find blackberries when they were in season. These were usually large plump ones, due to all the moisture being close by, and easy to gather as well, with the exception of the water snakes.

At other times, we'd be walking down in that crevice and run headlong into an arrogant ole cow with long horns who refused to move so we could get by. We'd yell at her, throw rocks, and if we could find a stick long enough, we'd bang on her. Finally she'd turn around slowly and move out so we could proceed downstream to a good place to climb out, till we found another occasion to go exploring.

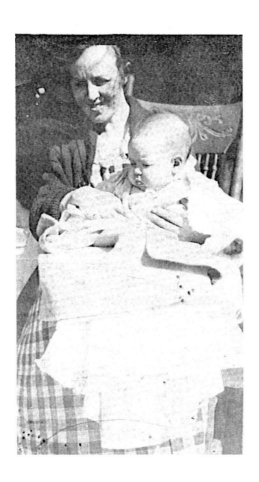

The Monumental Family Tree

Surely this magnolia tree wasn't 60 feet tall when it was planted, but that's the only way I can remember it.

The lower limbs had all been cut off to permit sweeping the leaves out from under the tree; consequently, after years of cleaning, a lot of big roots had been exposed. These harbored even more leaves and caused a lot of "stumped" toes. some of the kids would have as many as three "white" bandages on their feet at the same time. The white bandages were to cover the scraped and bleeding toe injuries. The wounds were seldom washed very good, but they had to be covered with salve and wrapped in a "white" bandage, which was white only till you got back out in the yard, but that was supposed to prevent infection and help with the healing.

There was really no way you could climb that tree in a hurry. The limbs were close together and very strong, but by the time you were six, you had mastered the art along with "skinning the cat," hanging on to a limb, putting your feet through your arms, turning loose and landing on your feet on the ground. Also there was this thing called "chinning the limb". This was accomplished by grabbing a limb taller than yourself and pulling up till your chin hung over the limb. Not to appear; a weakling or a "rotten egg," you practiced this art till you mastered it, even though it took months, a bunch of skinned elbows and bumped legs and fannies.

For all occasions this tree was the center of attraction for all ages. The older kids climbed to the top, the younger ones settled on the limbs progressively lower down the trunk, while the toddlers scrambled around on the ground falling over the roots and "squalling" because they couldn't climb up. Having the luck of the Irish, no one ever fell any distance from the tree or got a real injury playing in it. This "God Sent" tree was the perfect hiding place for those who chose not to be found, and it was also a dreamer's paradise. There was an awful lot of imagination wasted up there amongst those leaves and limbs, looking out over the whole yard, all the out-houses, cemetery and paths, and even at some of the neighbors' houses.

Our mother often praised the Lord that we had only one magnolia tree, especially when the large, tough leaves started shedding and we had to sweep them up in a pile and carry them out to the edge of the yard.

The Delicacy Of Delicacies:
"Homemade Ice Cream"

Ice cream parlors were non-existent in our area when I was a kid. There were a few places where you could buy ice cream, but with roads as bad as they were and cars as scarce as they were and money almost non-existent, we mostly made our own with whatever we had on hand.

As soon as the weather got hot enough and the barefoot season opened up, we'd get a great urge for some homemade freezer ice cream (hand cranked style).

Often we'd only have one cow giving milk at the time, and it was hard to sacrifice the whole lot (butter and all) to use it for that purpose. However, if we found enough change to pay for the ice and a volunteer to go get it, we'd get the process underway.

Our Dad liked bananas or banana flavoring, but most of us would have liked another flavor, except that we didn't have much choice, so we usually made banana ice cream. It really didn't matter what flavor you put in it, it seldom killed the wild onion or bitter weed taste, resulting from what the cow had eaten all day. The best thing it had going for it was that it was cold and we could tell it was sweet. '

The big ole gallon and half freezer took forever to "make". We all took turn grinding; some of us would sit on top to steady the freezer, and it took one person fulltime picking away on the big chunk of ice to keep adding little pieces of ice to that melting in the freezer. In real hot weather it melted so fast we'd hardly have enough ice to freeze the milk, especially after everyone kept snitching little chunks to put down each other's collar.

Eventually it was ready to eat (readiness was judged by how hard it was to (turn the crank). If it was impossible to turn any more, it was time to sound the alarm about it being ready to eat.

In preparation for serving there had been stacked on a nearby table a dozen dessert dishes, spoons, and a long-handled serving spoon and napkins, if we had any paper ones. Once the top was removed from the freezer we had to exercise extreme caution not to drip salt water on the top of the cream; when that happened, the first two servings were almost ruined, but you didn't throw it away for any reason.

The mamas and papas were served first, as at any meal, as though the little kids had a world of patience and didn't get hungry. By the time all of the dishes had been filled it was time to start over with refills. We dipped and ate as long as it lasted. Whether you'd had plenty to eat didn't even figure into the situation; you just ate as long as there was any.

Sometimes you would get so cold eating fast you'd have to go find a wrap to cover up with, the unfortunate ones who had to clean up wondered if it was worth all the trouble. The salt in the bottom of the freezer was hard to wash out, especially when there was little available water. As customary, the salt water in the bottom was to be poured on the Bermuda grass, in hopes it would kill it, or at least stunt its growth, and no matter what the time, no matter if it was dark or light, all this procedure had to be adhered to; right down to the last drip of water.

The Saga Of The Mad Dogs

Ever since I can remember we were indoctrinated with scary stories about mad dogs. At that time dogs were not inoculated to prevent rabies (either because we couldn't afford it or the knowledge had not reached our neck of the woods),and once an animal had this most horrendous disease and infected another, a tortuous and sure death followed shortly thereafter.

A lot of animals in our area had contracted rabies at one time or another, and consequently died or had to be killed. Whenever a hog or cow had been bitten they would be kept in a pen till it could be determined if they were really going mad.

At any rate, we were warned to take cover, head for the house or barn, slam the doors or climb trees if we saw an unfamiliar dog approaching. Back then, everybody's dogs wandered around. Some of them got carried away hunting rabbits or foxes and ran a long way from home in hot pursuit. As soon as they lost track of the animal or caught it they'd head for home. They then took the short cuts back which inevitably led through someone's back yard.

Naturally the old dogs weren't familiar with all those mad dog tales, so they'd just trudge on toward home, exhausted. Usually their heads and tails would be tucked to show humility, since they were in a strange territory. But ... those two characteristics were also some of the sure signs of rabies. As soon as one was spotted everyone started yelling "madog" (short for mad dog). Without ever seeing the mongrel to recognize him as belonging to a neighbor everyone in hearing distance would sound the alarm "madog" till half the community was running for cover and a loaded gun.

When the men folks got a good look at him they could tell instantly who he belonged to and that cleared the poor old dog. But, about the time he got out of sight another one would come sashaying by. However, if he

94

wagged his tail and wore a kind of smile on his face he was cleared for passage. Otherwise, we went through the same ritual of warning all the folks in the neighborhood about the possible danger. In the summer there weren't many days that we didn't go through the mad dog scare. Rabies was the "cancer" or "heart attack" of our day nothing was more serious!

In the spring we'd ride on a wagon with our bare feet dangling off the back. When we'd pass a house the dogs would come running out to the road barking and chasing the mules. This, of course, triggered the panic button. We'd yank our feet up and back in the wagon in a hurry.

When we were out in the fields at work, if and when we'd see a strange dog approaching, we would almost instantly panic. Some of our elders had warned us to be real still or lie down away from the dog's trail, assuming they could not see or smell very well, but we were much too frightened to do a thing like that. We were indeed fortunate not to have to make that decision.

Whenever our visits at night involved a lot of walking we sure put the speed on at the thought of a mad dog or an unusual sound. Our imagination really ran away with us on such occasions.

If a neighbor had a dog, cow, or pig go mad they'd pen him up good and tight and let the whole neighborhood come and see them. They were a most frightening sight, slobbering and growling or snarling and butting their head against the walls. We just had to see them! We didn't have many horror movies back then, but this experience sufficed for all of us excitement seekers.

Everyone tried real hard to keep their dearest pets close by so we could rescue them if need be. When my oldest sister was about four years old she was playing with her baby brother on the porch when she saw a strange acting dog coming into the yard. She dragged the baby into the house and slammed the door just as the real mad dog leaped up on the porch. Our Mother told us this story repeatedly to keep us reminded of the real danger involved.

95

Some people with strong imaginations and a free play on the truth, related some wild experiences about their narrow escapes. We loved to hear them all, real or imagined, and most especially about a man in the community who really went mad and suffered untold agony till he finally died.

Saving The Chewing Gum

I don't believe I would have ever made it in this life if someone hadn't discovered chewing gum. This craze started when I was very young and was so embedded, I'd even clean up my kid brothers' shoes for a "block" of gum (we may have been the only people in captivity who referred to a stick of gum as a block, but we did).

When you had extra pennies to use on a luxury, it was agonizing to choose whether to put them all on a pack of gum, or get a bag of candy, or buy a "dope" (cola); about half the time we'd decide on gum (Juicy Fruit). This was not an item that you passed around or shared in any capacity, it was more like an item that you kept a secret and hid, if it were possible.

We didn't chew it a little while and discard it, we only took it out of our mouth to eat, at which time we stored it under the table top where we sat, and then put it (or what we thought was it) back in our mouth immediately following the meal. It had a permanent home in our mouths unless if by some sad misfortune it dropped out and got too much dirt to be cleaned off. Our other main storage spot was the bed headboard. After a while they got all crudded over where we'd used the same spot over and over. On occasions our Mother would make us scrape it all off and clean the headboards, but it wasn't long till we were right back in business as usual in the same spots.

Every now and then a smaller kid would snitch someone's gum off the headboard and that would really create havoc, as we'd naturally go down the line taking the little wads off in succession till we ran out and someone's was missing. As soon as we found the culprit we'd take it away from him, wash it off real good and everyone was happy 'cept the thief.

In the first place we hated to part with our gum when we went to bed at night, and consequently, one of us would go to sleep with it in his mouth. Somehow the gum would get a way and wound up, of all places, in our hair!

If you were totally unable to pull all the hair out of the gum by yourself, you'd have to call in reinforcements. First, one sister or Mom would work on it and then another, and finally that last resort would be inevitable - it had to be cut out with the scissors. We looked a little "buggy whipped" with a chunk cut out of our hair at a very obvious spot. Everyone knew what the deal was, unless you'd got it stuck in your bangs. Back then, a lot of little girls who got hold of some scissors would cut their own bangs at all angles and even up to the hair line in places. There was no way to cover up that mess, we just had to suffer through it, till it grew out.

When we had absolutely run out of gum, new or chewed and saved, we'd get a terrible hankering for something to chew on. At this time we'd take off in search of a sweet gum tree. These trees produced a resin that ran down the tree on the outside, and at certain times was toughened enough to be scraped off. This we put in our mouth and tried to chew the little chunks together. It was awfully crumbly and you'd labor for minutes trying to keep it all together so you could soften it up enough to chew. It had a wonderful taste. The only thing about sweet gum was, more times than not, it was gooey and too soft. It would have made wonderful glue, but we didn't need any glue, and we aimed to chew it, so we raked it off our fingers into our mouth and started working it up.

We'd uncover one tooth at a time and chew very lightly till we got it to resembling chewing gum. You'd chew for a few minutes with great satisfaction and then it would start getting hard, so much so that the back of your jaw would get sore; not only that, you had gotten your teeth so coated with the mess it took days to get it all brushed or scraped off. We weren't easily discouraged with the sweet gum. We did the same thing over and over, and regarding the chewing gum, the years didn't bring about much change in some of us either. We'd use any extra change we could come up with for some more of the uncomparable "Juicy Fruit" gum, and we'd guard it with great secrecy while our friends and playmates drooled.

Watermelon Cutting

We always had a watermelon patch. The latter was what we called the space where we planted the watermelons, and that could mean one long row or three short ones. Since the vines grew to such great proportions, the ground allowed for the patch covered a big area.

The seeds had to be planted at just the right time in order to harvest the melons around the 4th of July. Our Dad only planted Congos or Dixie Queens, which were usually dark green all over and bright red on the inside. There was a yellow-meat melon that some of our neighbors planted, and they were very sweet and mealy on the inside. However, we didn't like them nearly as well as the red-meat ones, plus we thought they just didn't really look right, so we stuck to the red ones.

Keeping the weeds and grass out of the patch was a terrible chore, 'cause you had to be careful about moving those long runners around to get the undergrowth out. We planted only what we thought we could eat with maybe a few extras, hoping they'd be bigger than our neighbors and we could carry them around and brag on them.

The way to tell when a melon was ripe was to thump on them. To me they all sounded alike, but those more experienced fanners could pick one out in a flash.

During the season we always kept two or three of the best ones laying around on the back porch so they'd be handy if and when we decided to eat one. Also, the best ones had a way of disappearing if you left them in the patches for very long. We ate ours in the afternoon or after supper. They were never served at mealtime.

When the entire group was assembled, mostly family, but occasionally some company, we'd move a table into place, gather up a batch of spoons or knives, a salt shaker (our Dad always put salt on his), place the chosen melon in the middle of the table, take our longest and sharpest butcher knife and start cutting. We always cut ours lengthwise, first in half and then divided into wedges three to four inches wide, depending on how many pieces we had to have to serve everyone. Every now and then we'd cut into one that wasn't quite ripe, and after passing around all the accusations as to who pulled one that wasn't ripe, we'd set it aside and try another one.

Oddly enough, we never ate these things except on the back porch or out in the yard. Of course, with "fifty-lebm" kids messing with them we should have understood why. In this way we could eat them as we pleased. Sometimes we'd bite them right from the rind, but mostly we'd cut out sections and eat them from our fingers, a very sticky and juicy process.

The blasted things had so many seeds one could take very few bites without having to de-seed the chunk. If I'd had any part in inventing the things I'd have placed all the seeds in a neat little wad at one end or the other instead of having them scattered all over the watermelon. However, those seeds made a wonderful game for us as soon as we had eaten our piece down to the rind.

We'd take the slippery little mischiefs between our thumbs and forefingers, aim at someone and release them, hoping they'd go forward and hit someone. Very seldom did they hit the target, but that made the game even more fun. If we had on good clothes we didn't play that, because they'd land all over you, including your hair. In the thick of the fight you'd have seeds coming at you from every angle. These games would last till we got tired and then we'd start cutting into the rinds to make some "false teeth."

Our Mother nearly always wanted the best parts of the rinds to make pickles and/ or preserves, so we had to get permission to waste the rinds. This procedure with the teeth started by cutting the slightly pink part into the white part, just above the green outside. We'd slice a thin wedge and cut little sections out to look kind a snaggle-toothed and just wide enough to fit into our mouths, with long front teeth hanging down. They were grotesque looking but were a lot of fun, as we compared dentures and laughed at each other's weird looks. Since they were downright miserable, to say the least, we didn't wear them for long.

By this time the flies and bees had discovered the festivities, so we had to start carrying the watermelon remains to the hogs, and then we poured water on all the juice and seeds that were on the ground. Our Mom handled her part of the rinds and cleaned off the table and carried the knives, etc., back in the house. It was somewhat of a relief for the watermelon season to be over. We never bought any, so we had them. only when ours got ripe or when our neighbors brought us one of theirs to "try" during hot weather.

The Dual Purpose Scuppernong Vines

It was a usual sight to see a large squarish framed-up scuppernong vine standing a little bit over "head tall" in everyone's back yard. We and all our neighbors had had them always, so it seemed, they kinda came with the house.

Even though the grapes were so seasonal and their crops so weather-controlled we always kept the large vines and just let nature take its course. We kids made good use of it as long as the weather was "fitten." We made a luxurious play house under it. The lovely thick-leafed vines made a perfect shade overhead and the long runners hanging over the sides of the frames offered a lot of privacy.

Our Mom and Dad never came to see what we were playing nor how much house wares we had carted out there from our house for our "playhouses." We even had a section for a beauty shop. Here we kept a pair of scissors which we used to trim our hair and even eyelashes and eyebrows if we could get to them.

The bangs were usually a dead give-away. There was so much squirming around, we just couldn't get those things cut straight. When our Mom got a look at that freakish trim, we'd have to relinquish the scissors, but with time we'd get them back and do a, little more trimming.

Our main playhouse even had bench seats that you could really sit on. Made with wood blocks and old planks- our little tables were old buckets or pans that had holes in the bottoms or the handles torn off. With all of our ideas we'd furnish all the laid-off rooms and then churn with our soap-sudsy fruit jars or sweep with our discarded all-straw brooms or just play with our Sears-Roebuck paper dolls. This occupied our time for hours till someone called us for lunch.

Then we'd often eat fast and go right back to playing right where we'd left off. We'd have a "pretend Mama" who gave all the orders and did most of the cooking. The leaves and twigs and green scuppernongs or hacked- up "sneaked" squash made a beautiful meal on our improvised plates of various discarded broken dishes.

In one spot we could even play hop-scotch if we moved our benches. If company came, we headed them straight to our scuppernong vine playhouse. This must have been a great "baby sitter" for our parents. They certainly never bothered us when we were under there.

The real purpose of the vine was kinda secondary to us, but we did enjoy those tasty grapes once they got ripe. With those little ravenous appetites running around, the poor scuppernongs barely got turned before we started sampling them. We ate them so green and acidy that they caused little red bumps to break out in and around our mouths. But the memory of that experience didn't last long, we'd do the same thing over and over.

In a good year there would be a cluster of large round tannish grapes in abundance hanging overhead and around the edges. When this happened, the whole family invaded our poor playhouse and all our wonderful "secret furnishings" got exposed. A few things got confiscated and returned to their rightful place in the main house, where we'd let them stay for a while before we resneaked them out.

During the late summer, when the fruits of the vines were fully ripe, we'd take any and all of our company to our scuppernong vine for refreshments and comparison purposes. We hoped they'd say ours were better than theirs. Everyone in the whole county was foundered on them when the frost finally came and finished them off but we had canned a lot of juice for winter and had that to remember them by.

The Fruit Drying Process

Since we didn't spray our fruit trees, we didn't have first class fruit. It was often wormy, rotted easily or was blight-stricken in other ways. Almost every year we had fruit of a sort and always made every effort to save it somehow. We always canned the best looking peaches, apples and pears, but there was more of the faulty fruit so we peeled, sliced and dried those small pieces (apples and peaches) to make fried pies when the fresh fruit was all gone.

First in the preparations, we'd peel and slice every little piece that could possibly be saved. Then we rigged up a table or some other flat surface out in the yard in full sun to try to dry them real fast. Often, we'd level up some tin roofing on two sawhorses, wipe it real clean, and spread each little piece out separately, hoping to let the air and heat circulate around them. When this space had all been used up, we'd spread brown papers on the edge of the porches or any other handy place that was in full sun.

Before we got half the fruit spread out, the bees and flies had already discovered it and from then on, it was a constant bat and knock situation trying to keep them away till we were through. Shortly after we'd spread it all out in the sun, we'd start turning each piece over so it could dry out on all sides as fast as possible. If it hadn't rained in a month, there was sure to come up a real fast, hard shower on the fruit, which sent us hurrying around trying to rescue it before it got drenched.

The bees and bugs were already into it by this time, and we worked like fury to rake them aside so they wouldn't sting us as we scraped up the tiny pieces to dump them in a big pan and carry inside. If and when it did get wet, we had to tumble the damp stuff around and spread it out on our dining table or on a bedspread all up and down the hall floor to keep it from spoiling or mildewing.

Sometimes this went on for days before the sun came out in full blast. The whole house wound up smelling like half-spoiled fruit. It certainly was a relief to have the sun put in an appearance so we could get the smelly stuff out of the house and start it to drying one more time. When the sun would shine for several days in a row the fruit would be dry in that length of time, but when it rained or was cloudy, it took a long time to get it all processed just right and ready for storing in a dry place.

What started out as gobs of sliced fruit, shrunk up to be only one big pan full when all the juice was dried out or evaporated there was hardly any fruit left. These small pieces were now minute. It took a lot of careful handling to pick it all up. But as soon as it was reasonably dry the bees and flies diminished, but the ant hung in there and had to be brushed off and aside. When the fruit had been completely dried, we took long shallow pans and spread it out to be heated in a warm oven for a certain length of time to kill the bug eggs or germs that it had absorbed during the drying process. Periodically, we'd remove the pans, stir the fruit and put it back in the oven to finish preparing it for storing.

We stored ours in large glass jars with brown paper in between layers to absorb moisture or in cloth bags which were made for this purpose. When the containers were properly sealed, this would keep the fruit for more than a year and that was a blessing.

It seemed real odd to spend so much time drying the fruit just to remove it from its dry place, wash it, add water to it and puff it right back up to where we started the process. This treasured fruit was mostly used for making those wonderful "fried pies," which had several other names such as "tarts" or "turnovers" and one family referred to them as "left and rights" having derived the name from the way the mother stacked them on the dish as she cooked them. The normal shape for them resembled a half-moon. Everyone loved them in spite of their thousands of calories and they weren't ever refused by anyone for any reason that I ever heard of.

The Original One-Size-Fits-All

Our mother was a genius at improvising. The lack of ingredients, tools, or in this case, patterns, never stopped her from achieving her goal or finishing a task. She didn't show any partiality when it came to making our drawers; all of them were just alike and almost all of them the same size, even though the girls ages ranged from three to twenty- five. There was no problem figuring out which was the front or back, they were just alike on both sides. The elastic in the waist and legs was good and loose, and the soft flannel material for winter or cotton broadcloth for summer was good and roomy.

We never figured out where she got her pattern, but after giving it a lot of thought, I think she just used an old shirt pattern, turned it upside-down, cut out the neck part, sewed it together, shortened the sleeves and made them a little larger and put elastic around what would have been the shirt tail bottom for the waist.

These homespun body covers did suffice but were often embarrassing to wear. For one thing, they simply wouldn't stay up neither the waist nor the legs!!!We were constantly yanking them up. You'd get behind everyone else and hurry and yank up one side or the other of the legs, and if time permitted the waist. Sometimes the slip or dress would get caught up on one side during the hasty procedure.

On one occasion, our grandmother sent us to the store with some brownish eggs to buy her some bath soap. She was very considerate and put in a couple of extra eggs so that we could get some candy for ourselves. Well, the eggs we were used to were white, and we'd become accustomed to hearing about "rotten eggs" so we decided to crack one or two to make sure she was sending "good eggs" to the store, thereby forfeiting our candy money. Enroute to the store (we always walked), drawers were a nuisance, always slipping down below our dress hems. We decided to remedy the situation by taking them off and hiding them under a bush until we came back down the path. Of course we were very self-conscious and shy about not having on any drawers, so we were very careful to hold our dresses down with our stiffened arms straight by our sides and hoped against hope that we didn't get in the middle of a whirlwind, which was quite common in that area at that time of year.

By-words:
Slang Or Personal Expressions

Slang words were a good way of expressing alarm, dismay, or dissatisfaction when your vocabulary was limited and you weren't the family of the clergy. There were a lot of older farmers who used profanity (taking the Lord's name in vain) and even vulgarity. They kept a lot of the worst sayings out of the "women folks'" hearing, but having a bunch of brothers as we did, some of them did get back to us girls.

Several sayings or expressions were generally associated with only one person. It must have been hard trying to think up an expression that hadn't already been used by someone else. Still, they tried. One ole fellow would be the originator and master of the old saying, "By George!"; another, "By Golly," and someone else, "By Granny," or "By gosh," "By cracky," "By dam," or "By Gravy," etc., with the by-words. Some others were noted for things like "Blame it," "Plague it," "Dammit," "Doggone it," "Dog bite it," "Blast it," "Dog June," "Dad gum," "I'll be dog-goned," or "Gosh-a-mighty."

Still a few others, with religious inclinations, would use those age old favorites, "The Lord as my witness," "Lawdy mercy," "Lawd hep us," "Land o' Goshen," "If the Lord's willin' and the creeks don't rise," "Holy cow," "Holy mackerel," "Holy Jehoshaphat," and "If the Good Lord's willin'." Then there was always some who had to have sanctions for their tales, or felt others might need convincing with such as: "To tell the truth," "I kid you not," "Cross my heart," "As sure as I'm a standing here," "No 27 ways about it," "As sure as shootin'," "Honest to goodness," "I hope to die," (Ain't that the truth, Goofus?"), "I ain't smart, but I know ... so and so."

The women had a few remarks that they used almost exclusively, like: "Silly goose," "Thunderation," "Land sakes," "Aw shucks," "Man alive," "So help me Hannah," "Well, I want to know," "I don't fault you," "You're joshing me," or "For the luv of Mike."

In response to an inquiry about yours or someone else's health or well-being, you'd often hear, "He's as sick as a dog," "Shore looks bad," "Ain't got no color," "Ain't long for this world," "On his last laig," "Pale as a ghost," "Thin as a rail," "Poorly," "Tolerable," "Not doing no good," "Fit to kill," "Fit as a fiddle," "Mighty low," or "Not worth a killing."

Funnier than most were the expressions used by parents threatening their children, and imagining what the poor kids thought in response. Often you'd hear an irate parent say, "Don't make me get up from here". Must have had a keen imagination; no one wanted them to get up. And then there were words such as, "I'm not gonna tell you again". What a relief, they'd already heard it a dozen times; "Do you want me to tell your Daddy?" Not really, I'd have told him, if I did; "Now shut your mouth and eat your food," reckon they wanted us to stuff it up our noses; "Don't talk till I tell you to". Can't you just hear them coming over and saying, "It's your time, now talk!"; "If you do that again I'll smack you clear across the room". Must have been stronger than they looked; "I'll wear you out". No doubt about it, in conversation if no other way; "Do that again and I'll tear you up". Imagine growing up and wondering how many pieces they're gonna make out of you; "If you don't stop that I'll jerk a knot in your tail". Real flattering, thought you were a cat or a monkey; " If I ever catch you doing that again I'll whip the tar out of you". That must be what held your bones together back them; "You ain't a tellin' me what to do". All of the conversations were strictly one-sided back then; kids were to be seen and not heard; "You do as I say not as I do," - Hmmnn, he was bigger.

Some of the funniest things you could hear if you were a listener were the critical comparisons with no offense intended, for instance:

"She was as *pretty as a picture.*"
"That old man was as *ugly as homemade sin.*"
"She was as *fat as a cow.*"
"He was as *big as an elephant.*"
"The postman is *as slow as a snail*"

"Their dog was *as fast as a bullet*."
"Their son *ate like a horse*."
"Her baby *slept like a log*."
"That ole maid would talk the *horns off a Billy goat*."
"She had a face that would *stop a freight train*."
"Pore Dad was as *tired as a horse*."
"Sister was as *sick as a buzzard*."
"He ain't got enough sense to *get out of a shower of rain*."
"That boy *smelled like a Billy goat*. "
"That little girl is *growing like a weed*"
"Her teacher was as *smart as a whip*."
"His kid was as *sharp as a tack*."
"The storm was over as *quick as a flash* "
"The mail man is as *slow as Christmas*. "
"'Twas over before you could say *"Jack Robinson*."
"Lula was as crazy as a *Betsy bug*."
"Their oldest son was as *wild as a buck*."
"The weeds were as *thick as hops*."
"Up there it's as cold as *blue blazes*."
"There were as many flies as *Carter sowed oats*."

We Had A Tobacco Chewer

Nearly every family in our community had a tobacco user of some description. Some of them had one or two snuff dippers, a couple of smokers and a tobacco chewer. We didn't have any snuff dippers but several smokers and one nasty tobacco chewer.

Before the word got out about how bad tobacco was for your health, every man was smoking by the time he was 14-16 years old. My old grandmother certainly never knew about that health hazard either, because she smoked a cob pipe, off and on, till she died at 99 years old.

We didn't grow much tobacco in our area but a bunch of it was used and sold in cans, bags, packs, twists, and the real popular plugs (the type my Dad used). It was real common place for these farmers to roll their own cigarettes from a can of "Prince Albert" or a bag of "Bull Durham." This they'd brandish from their overall back pockets and proceed to dig the rolling paper from their front bib pockets of their overalls. They retrieved only one piece of paper, opened the can or bag of tobacco and dumped a little pile of tobacco in the middle of it. As soon as they had fastened the tissue thin paper together around the tobacco, they'd lick the edges to hold the roll together, then rake a wood stick match across their overalls, to light it up.

Many men had rolled so many cigarettes that they could master the act with just one hand. They all had tobacco breath and every house smelled with tobacco smoke, especially in the winter when the windows and some doors were closed. Even with all the unpleasantness, it seemed to be an all-around tranquilizer for most of them and nothing was ever said about kicking the habit.

The cigarette smoking was nearly as annoying as the tobacco chewing; that really got on your nerves. Nearly all of the older men kept a plug of "Brown Mule" chewing

111

tobacco in their overall pockets. It was routine to bite off a big chunk after meals or mid-morning and afternoons.

In the wintertime, Dad would always sit as close to the fireplace as he could and use it for a spittoon. We'd stay as far away as we could in case he spattered us or missed his aim. In the summer, he parked his chair real close to the edge of the porch so he could spit out into the yard, except for the few dribbles that usually fell on the floor, his aim was very good after 50 years of practice. To master the art, he'd put his index and middle fingers about an inch apart and spit between them for a fairly long distance and was pretty accurate with hitting the target. Fortunately, he didn't carry a spit cup around with a napkin in it, as many of the men did back then. That was so unsightly that it was nauseating.

When we went visiting, the older men would often sit on the porch, even in cool weather, and chew tobacco and spit in unison while they talked. That was a good arrangement for the women folk who were spared this gross procedure at least till they got home. Whenever you'd see two or three old men walking around, you'd see them yank out that old tobacco plug and pass it around. Without missing a step, they'd continue on with their inspection of the garden or crops, talking, making hand motions, and spitting as they walked.

Chewed tobacco was not all bad cause it was recommended for insect bites. For this use, you took a small amount of moistened, softened tobacco and plastered it directly on the sting or bite and sometimes it seemed to draw the poison out. The other good quality was the juice could be used to kill worms or bugs of some sort on some garden plants. It sure took a lot of observing and thinking to recognize the good in that horrendous procedure.

Beloved Paths

Where I lived paths were as much a part of the scenery as the houses. There must have been a dozen paths around our place, all kept clean with use. Paths were then and are now a very appealing sight to me. In fact, I think they are one of nature's most intriguing possessions. In some cases it seemed to me there was some sort of sanctuary at the path's end.

Most of our paths were very necessary and connected two important places. They were used often and usually for specific purposes. One of our most traveled was the one that led to our aged grandmother's house. We ran or skipped over that crooked little path a million or more miles, carrying her meals or other necessary items. We never attempted to use it after dark because it was so rough. This trail had a heavy "foot log" type bridge which spanned a fairly deep gully. This really kept us in good shape balancing as we hurried across it. On occasion we'd see if we could cross it with something balanced on our heads.

Each sunny day we'd scan the bushes and weeds for a young rabbit or squirrel or anything out of the ordinary so we would have something exciting to tell when we got home.

Another path we kept "hot" was the one that led to the spring where we got a lot of our drinking water, did the family wash, and took slop to the hogs, as well as the path that enabled us to stop off at the barn to milk the cows. In the summertime we also used this path to go to the spring to take our weekly baths.

The water was icy cold, so I'm sure we performed some very fancy motions trying to hurry and keep ourselves warm. Years later we learned that the bachelors in our neighborhood hid in the woods and watched. If we had known we could have charged for the show. After all, some of us didn't look so bad and there were several of us.

113

The path to the large family toilet was second to none in popularity. This was a big hangout for the chickens, so we'd have to scare them out of our trail as we went. Often two of us would use it at the same time, since the building would accommodate as many as three at one time. Here we could exchange secrets and talk about everybody else as we thumbed through the catalogues. We could stay there as long as we pleased 'cause no one ever called us out of there!

There was also a path that some of our neighbors used that went smack through our yard. In the summer, or in good weather, we were always outside or on the porches, so our neighbors felt very obligated to engage in conversation as they walked by. They would tip their hats and speak to each person individually, even though it often took a good 20 minutes to complete the ritual. But, such was the custom, so it was both expected and appreciated. On these occasions we'd inquire about everyone's health, the weather, condition of the crops, and then any news that we'd heard on the telephone. This was mostly to verify its authenticity.

The path that interested us kids a lot was the one that led across a small stream of water, which we tiptoed through or stepped on scattered rocks to keep from getting our feet wet. This one took us to our favorite peach tree, and a few feet further to a huge currant bush, often housing a nest of baby birds, which we'd minutely inspect from their tiny beaks to their sharp toenails. These were the pleasure trips, but this was also the path to some cotton and corn patches where we spent a lot of dreaded times. In early spring when the fields were being prepared for planting we carried water to the men along this same route.

At another angle from our yard was a path that led us to a road where we went to visit several different families. These families had kids about our ages, and we loved to visit them at certain times of the year, usually to take advantage of their scuppernongs and pecans. Also, some of these kids were real good at hatching up new games to play. We'd play good and be real agreeable for a while and then we'd get mad and go home.

114

In the pastures there were many other paths that the cows and mules had made. They carried a lot of excitement for us, as we traveled them all to see where they led and why. On some of these trails we discovered some minnows in the branch, or found some mistletoe up in a tree, or a good crabapple tree; or if we were lucky a hickory nut tree with a bunch of hickory nuts under it. To take full advantage of such a find we'd find a big rock and a smaller one, gather up several nuts and place one on the big rock while we pounded it with the small rock. The nuts were so smashed we could hardly tell which was the meat and which the hull. Nevertheless, we struggled around with it, trying to unlodge some of the good stuff, until we'd finally give up and go looking for something else

There was also a good long path that led over a hill through a densely wooded area to our Aunt's house. We didn't visit her that much but she had a granddaughter who visited her regularly, and because there was no one for her to play with there she'd use that path to come over to our house. This trail always looked a little "boogery" so we hurried along over it expecting to be attacked by some ferocious animal. The bushes and briars had grown so much from one summer to the next, we kinda' had to shove our way through. This path was used only in daylight hours, due to the wooded darkness.

The "path of boredom" was the one that led to our family cemetery. It wasn't very far from our house, and the patches between our house and that graveyard kept the view cleared so we could see it from our front porch. When the day's work was over and we had nothing better to do we'd wander out in that direction where several other family members would join up.

Before we returned we'd have struck up a lively conversation and begun to sing, or we'd start racing each other back to the house. At any rate, that was a memorable path also.

The Medicine Shows

With hard times and the scarcity of money prevailing all over the country, it was unbelievable that we even had an influx of out-of-state traveling medicine shows come to our community. Of course they were en route somewhere else (anywhere that looked halfway prosperous) and gave every indication that they themselves were gypsy or hobo style wanderers.

They traveled in a motorized covered wagon half full of so called medicine and sticks of solder. The company consisted of no more than three people, a scant change of clothes, a few cooking utensils, a musical instrument of some sort, and sometimes a little dog.

When the truck turned the corner toward the community stores, it created a lot of excitement. Most of the time they would stay beside my Dad's old store, which was not in full operation. As soon as they'd set up headquarters (which must have taken all of five minutes), they'd start mingling around with the local yokels at and around the store and cotton gin.

They had a different look and spoke in a foreign (to us) lingo. Everyone in the community treated them like royalty. As soon as the school kids and women heard about their arrival they'd all hurry around and make plans to attend each and every show.

 The show would start just before dark. The audience sat on a cleared out spot of ground, and we all brought something for the "collection," often we'd bring a bag of potatoes, or onions, or a chicken or eggs, or any other thing we could think up. Very few coins were collected. I imagine they got a good collection of buttons, because it was dark and one couldn't tell what was dropped in the hat till it got to a good light. Guess they got enough coins to buy the gas for they came back time and again.

The shows themselves were very light fare and one would be hard put to label them entertainment. If there had been any other form of amusement I'm sure we would not have gone at all.

The entertainers (the owners) must have been retired circus performers, or so it seemed. They'd don a wig, whip out a harmonica, clown around and sing some original song or tell a few jokes, or dance a tacky jig - all of which preceded the sales pitch for the medicine.

At most they'd have three different kinds of merchandise to sell. Usually one medicine was claimed to be a cure for everything from hiccups to an in-grown toenail. If it didn't agree with you and you couldn't take it internally, it could even be used as a "liniment" for external application, and if that didn't work you could fumigate or disinfect with it. Also, if you bought two bottles you'd get a stick of solder "free." This solder was very valuable for mending enamel coated pans, dippers, and buckets, which were always developing leaks or rusted through places where the enamel was thin. So everyone tried real hard to round up enough money to buy either the liquid medicine or the salve type just to get the solder.

As soon as they realized the crowd had no more money to spend they'd continue with the "super duper" program. They saved the best part of the show till the last so no one would leave till they had passed around "that hat" at intermission.

We could hardly wait for them to come back out to the forefront (there were no stages) to get on with the show. This time they had memorized the lines which they'd direct to each other, like a real play. Then they'd sing some ole familiar song accompanied by a guitar or accordion. They'd even have a little dog to entertain every now and then. One of the men would dress up like a woman and perform; this brought a big happy response from the crowd. Sometimes they'd even come out with a different outfit on and we were mesmerized by such a wonderful extravaganza.

When the time came to go home we'd catch each other by the hand, guarding our stick of solder, clinch our medicine in the other hand and start feeling our way

117

home along the dark, dusty, rutted roads, all the while making plans to come back the next day. On the way, we'd repeat the jokes and try to sing those new songs.

After the second night they always left town. These guys were too smart to stay in one spot for over two nights. They could tell they had taken the locals for all their ready cash by then. So, they'd move on down the road a few miles till they found another community waiting with open arms and plan to return again within six months or at most the next year.

When Court Was In Session

Word spread quickly when there was to be court in our county. The elderly (or what looked elderly) men scanned the local newspaper to be sure of the time and who the lucky chosen ones were to appear for duty. In case there were any doubts in their minds, they'd go to the store and ask everybody there all the who's and where's and other particulars of the events.

Some of our close neighbors, only men, were always summoned for jury duty and our dad was the bailiff for this particular period. The "select" would gather at the community store and iron out all the pertinent details, the greatest of which was the transportation. He who had a running automobile with decent tires and a valid tag was nominated and unanimously approved to furnish the transportation. All of the others met at his house and chipped in to buy the gas.

The women folks hopped right onto their duty and washed and starched the husbands' white Sunday shirts and got out the ole press cloths and repressed those good navy serge pants. These poor trousers had been around for years and had never been commercially cleaned. Since they were wool, they certainly had never been washed either. When the occasion arose, they just got pressed over one more time and were considered ready for action. The fact that they were a little tighter and a little shorter each time wasn't even noticed by most people.

When the "D-Day" came, these men would rise early, eat a hearty breakfast, and set out to that designated meeting place where they'd sit or fidget around on the porch till it was time to move out. You weren't late for this occasion, so you got started in plenty of time to allow for a "blowout" or any other such mishap that might occur. These ole fellars were full of anxiety. Seeing all those other jurors and lawyers and defendants and plaintiffs plus the judge was more exciting than almost any other thing they'd ever done before.

119

When they arrived in town, they looked the whole place over (all five stores, service station, cafe, and newspaper office) before they settled down at the courthouse where they sat around and whispered until it was time to go inside for the real action. My dad was always a good listener and an even better critic. He remembered most of the things that were done along with who did them and found fault with any and everything that had any. Some of the things he'd repeat when he got home and others he remembered later and entertained us with them. We all enjoyed court week.

There were very few cases to be tried in that area; everybody did what was right to the best of his knowledge and the local fist fights, which were common in that day, settled a lot of disputes. The fact that you'd be turned out of the church for almost any reason at all kept a lot of peace in the camp. Especially with everyone belonging to one church or another and knowing all about each other's business.

On occasions, there'd be a land line dispute when someone died or when a tenant would move away carrying an extra cow or mule with him that would precipitate court action. Otherwise, there were very few reasons for court sessions.

At one hearing, two of our neighbors were asked to testify. Of course, this incurred all kinds of apprehension about the proper way to act and present your story without appearing to be ignorant or backwards. When the proceedings got underway and the first nervous neighbor was asked to give his account of the incident, he did so and sat down after which the second even more nervous neighbor was called up for his rendition of the same incident. To this, he replied, "Well brethren, my tale is just like brother Smith's. At this time, my dad said there was considerable silence.

On another day, an old gentleman practically turned his chair over squirming around trying to keep from going to the toilet but as nature would have it, he was forced to make a hasty departure, telling only the bailiff the

120

reason. As soon as the word got to the judge, all operations were halted till which time the departed brother saw fit or was able to return some time later. At another session, some of the spectators took a good close seat where the jury panel was to have been seated and had to be escorted to other seats.

One long lanky ole gentleman, a court regular, had a very distinctive way of sitting in his chair, with his legs crossed and the upper leg wrapped back around the lower leg. On this particular day, he had on a pair of shoes with a hole in the bottom that attracted a lot of attention before he noticed what all the stares were about.

During a lunch break over at the cafe, mention was made of the latest Baptist convention, where several of the group had been in attendance. The convention was held in another and larger town that had a hotel. When asked about the crowds and the sleeping facilities, one of the old gents 'lowed as how it was a little crowded, hardly enough beds to sleep everyone. This remark drew a ready response from one of the Methodist brethren who figured that as narrow as the Baptists were (referring to the closed communion) that they could have slept 4-6 to a bed.

Many of the court terms were completely foreign to most of the locals, so there was an enormous amount of repetition and explaining going on at all times. Hearing aids were non-existent back then and with the windows opened up and the loud talking on the outside along with the terrible acoustics inside, it was hard, at best, to hear what was going on. Most of the involved were not very educated and it took close concentration to decipher the pronunciation and phraseology that was being used.

When court was dismissed for the day, everyone had to stand around on the outside, light up a cigarette or get a chew of tobacco, and rehash all of the goings on 2-3 times each. There was no particular hurry to go home as all the farm chores had been reassigned to other family members and they themselves would definitely be wearing the same clothes again tomorrow. So, if the good

Lord was willing and the Creeks didn't rise, they'd be there as sure as shootin'.

Homework, Or A Reasonable Facsimile

Some of the happiest days were the ones we spent hurrying home from school with no homework. These days were few and far between after the second grade, but there were some. This idle time gave us time to play outside or set up our paper-doll house on the inside.

If it were cold weather, our time outside was very limited. A few rounds of jump rope or marbles or kick the ball would about do it, but on the inside, we could drag out those shoe boxes of paper-dolls, along with the homespun cardboard furniture, and play till our mother sent us outside to bring in firewood or come to supper. On the other hand, and on far more occasions, we had that everlasting homework to contend with.

For these times, almost all of us gathered around a big round table in the hall or the long dining table in the dining room and spread out our books, got a knife, and sharpened our penny pencils with the erasers worn off. Then we got as close as we could to the lamps so we could tell where the work began.

We loved to get the spelling done first. It was easy and the sentences we had to make with the words didn't have to be too brilliantly created. One of our older brothers, who had already learned too much to go to school, was anxious to help us with those sentences: They were incredible and the teacher recognized his style instantly, but she enjoyed them as much as we did.

Math always bogged us girls down. After we used up all ten fingers and made little addition marks on everything nearby, it got real hard to figure. We just assumed it was too demanding to take time to learn those multiplication tables and the simple little addition figures. At least two thirds of the errors in all our homework was in Math.

The reading assignments were a nuisance. Often it took several minutes to stumble through it and even then we seldom knew what we had read. We'd spell the hardest words out loud and everyone sitting around gave us a different pronunciation so it was kinda' like multiple choice picking the one you liked the best.

Geography was a hard word for us to learn. We'd call it anything from 'Geofregy" to "Geografrie." At the time it was of no immediate value to us, since we'd never been out of the country and neither had the teacher. We didn't have globes so we couldn't locate the places that we were studying and no one knew how to describe the people who lived there nor their customs, let alone the geographical aspects. We just hurried through that class so we could get on to bigger and better things. She did make us learn the states and their capitals which took the whole year and were much easier to forget.

History was very dull and those dates were very hard to remember. We were told nothing at school or at home to associate those dates with, so the years and events all ran together with very little emphasis placed on anything. We did leave grammar school knowing about Columbus and our first president and maybe the names of Lewis and Clark, but most of the things were memorized just for the monthly tests and then immediately forgotten thereafter.

To answer the questions at the back of the chapters, we'd have to review the pages time and again and then still miss a bunch of them. The lack of concentration accounted for some of the lack-a-daisical homework. As soon as we found our assigned places and all the needed items, someone would sneak out and come back with an apple or some peanuts or something else to eat and of course that set off a chain reaction. Everyone had to go find something to eat.

Someone else would have some chewing gum which they'd start pulling back and forth out of their mouth or another one would start twirling his hair while someone else would make funny sounds with his mouth or tapping his fingers on the table top. At any rate, it was hard to keep your mind on your business.

We tried not to waste any paper as our Dad fussed about us using so much paper, at the very best. Often we'd write on the backs of the pages or erase small amounts that had been written the day before and use that page again. The pencils that still had erasers were kept busy passing all around the table, erasing everyone's mistakes. The rubber was especially good to chew on, but we needed to save it to erase with, so we refrained from that. We really needed those scarce pencils that were about one-third rubber tips. Guess they hadn't been invented back then. Most of us had a habit of chunking our pencil lead in our mouth to write so the writing would be plainer. No one knew that lead would turn out to be harmful.

When it was finally bedtime, we'd tear out the pages of our efforts from our tablets, fold them together, long-wise down the middle, write our names and the subjects on the top lines, and poke 'em in the proper books. After piling all of our books together in our special stack, we'd hit the sack, ready for school the next day. We weren't very proud of our homework, but at least it was something to hand in and the teacher was very lenient to those who'd made an effort.

Cooking On The 'Wood' Stove

There weren't any "wood stoves" in our area, nor any other, but there certainly were wood-burning stoves which were referred to as "wood stoves." They were huge, heavy, sturdily built iron multipurpose stoves with an upper story and a big smoke stack on the back.

Some of them were attractively colored and some had their own personality by being built a little bit differently. Basically, they were made for cooking, but they also served other purposes, like heating the kitchen and dining areas, heating water for all household purposes, heating irons for the weekly ironing rituals, and often just to heat up food that had already been cooked and had to be recycled for another chance to get rid of it.

These big essential pieces of equipment were built with reservoirs on one side to hold water, while it had an upper deck to hold and keep warm foods that had already been cooked. They had large ovens with two permanent racks and four eyes that were really big removable lids built so as to allow for rearranging the wood sticks underneath in order to adjust the heat - to a degree. A damper was always built in to keep the draft from the stove pipes making too big a blaze. It was opened to start a fire and partially closed when the fire was burning well.

There was a little hinged flap on the side of the stove where you placed the wood sticks and newspapers or kindling to get the fire underway. After about three or four long-burning fires, the ashes would have to be removed so as to allow for air circulation in that area. These ashes were taken out with great care and put around the rose bushes or on the vegetable garden or around the pecan trees.

Each stove was placed on a large metal sheet so that sparks from the fire or dropped ashes would not burn the wood floors underneath. In the coldest winter weather the cats would establish a nesting place right behind the stove, which was placed diagonally across a corner in the kitchen to prevent the walls from getting too hot and making the stove's cooking area more accessible. There were occasions when mama cats brought their babies into the world right there behind the cooking stove.

A large wood box (a container that was really made out of wood) was normally placed real near the stove so as to be handy for rekindling the fire. Every now and then it would get half filled up with bark and small chips from the wood, at which time it had to be carried outside and emptied. Its contents had to be inspected carefully to see if a spoon or lifting pad or anything else of value had been dropped in there.

The job of filling that wood box fell to the youngest children, who could get up and down the back door steps. No matter what important thing they were doing at the time when Mom yelled for someone to go get some stove wood, they had to drop everything and run. That job just kept on going as we had to cook big breakfasts, even bigger dinners, and relatively large suppers. There were very few leftovers at our house; what the humans didn't eat, the hungry dogs and hogs did.

The cooking was not the only reason we had to keep the fires going. There was always a need for warm water for baths or mopping the floors and windows as well as washing that mountain of dishes, pots and pans that got messed up during every meal. Also, the ironing took its toll on that firewood. Every garment plus the bed linens and everything else that was fabric had to be ironed - by decree from the mother of the household. In short, there was very little time when someone wasn't bringing in wood and stoking that fire.

Our woodpiles were soon depleted and the men folks spent a lot of their time whacking down trees and sawing them up in proper length blocks to be split up several times so they would fit in the stove. When they got started on that job they'd often split up a big pile of wood before they stopped. We enjoyed watching them, so we busied ourselves with piling the little sticks neatly or stacking some of it on the porch so we could be close by to observe the accurate aims with the axes.

As the wood dried out, bugs would get on the sticks or under it, and occasionally we'd find an earthworm, of which we were deathly afraid. Our Mother often warned us to watch for snakes, as the woodpile got closer to the ground. She didn't really have to warn us 'cause we had already thought of that when we found those long wriggly earthworms under those other sticks.

Bringing in the wood would not have been such a nuisance if we hadn't had to contend with that infernal smart alecky ole tom turkey. He knew we were afraid of him, so he'd catch us squatting down or stooping over picking up wood and start strutting and side-stepping up real close to us as he made those awful sounds to be sure we saw him. We hated his guts and would swat him with a piece of wood if he got close enough. When our Mom heard those encounters she'd yell at us to stop banging on her turkey, even though he had relentlessly tried to attack us. It was a real pleasure watching him strut off toward the cow pasture away from us.

When the kitchen stove got all fired up it was really hot. All of the food had to be watched carefully or it would scorch or just plain burn up. We ate ever so many burned top or bottom biscuits for that very reason. The heat could not be adjusted, so every item you cooked required your undivided attention. If one of us got in the way when our Mom smelled her bread burning it was too bad; we got shoved aside while she rescued the bread.

Several times we'd accidentally touch the "red hot" stove and get burned or get our clothes too close and they'd get scorched. Mostly we didn't play nor go too close to that heated monster which was no respecter of persons.

When we had finished our weekend cleaning and mopped the kitchen floor we were always instructed to polish up the stove, which was accomplished by rubbing grease over the entire surface, which looked good for a short time but burned off with a smoke as soon as it was hot.

A Tribute To Granny

My Granny was one of a kind;
  She walked and talked with a cane.
She lived and worked during the Civil War,
  With Rebel blood in every vein.

She didn't have much in the way of beauty,
  But her heart was full of affection.
When danger approached she'd shoulder her gun,
  But her yell was her real protection.

Her trademark, if she had one,
  Was her faded and worn sunbonnet,
  About which I'm pretty sure
  there never was written a sonnet.

Her cooking methods were strictly unique
  and so was some of her cooking.
She could peel and boil and fry and bake
  without a whole lot of looking.

The lack of proper pots and pans
  presented no special worry;
She just used what was nearest at hand
  when she was in a hurry.

She visited around with neighbors,
Sharing vegetables, fruits, and gossip.
  She never knew the hardships
  of blown fuses nor leaking faucets.

Her cleaning device was simple,
A long-strawed, short-handled broom,
But it dusted and beat and knocked and chased
  everything there was in the room.

Money was no joking matter back then,
  She almost never had any,
And being as hard as it was to make,
  She watched each and every penny.

Mostly she kept her money bag

stored safely away in her bosom,
But some of her bills were kept
in her hose just so's she wouldn't lose 'em.

In Spring was the time to get doctored up
with sulphur and molasses;
Poke salit was cooked, while tallow for sores
was used on lads and lasses.

To sew something special for grandpaw
was one of Grann's delights,
'And with or without a pattern,
She had something whipped up by night.

She lambasted away with her needle
a-piling up the stitches,
Cause it didn't matter about the fit,
She was only making Grandpaw some britches.

To get a new catalogue once a year
was an accomplishment, not luck.
What she couldn't find in her almanac,
She could order from Sears Roebuck.

They had everything she could think of
and some things she never had seen.
Grandpaw was embarrassed at some of the things,
But those only made Granny beam.

She didn't have time for just sitting,
'Cept when she was quilting or knitting
or churning the clabbered milk for butter,
The thoughts of which made her shudder.

She seemed content in them quiet pore times
As she tended the animals and chickens,
Working and sweating all over the place
as she constantly fussed like the dickens.

But beneath that rugged and worn exterior
was a heart of gold with wisdom superior.
She lived and slaved for her children all,
No task for them was too big nor too small.

130

A great debt of gratitude we all owed her,
Although those thoughts didn't often occur.
We hope against hope she can finally know
that we think of her often as we live and grow.

Discipline According To The Bible

"Spare the rod and spoil the child," was one portion of the Bible that all of the parents during my childhood treasured and abided by. Nothing was said about loving your child and trying to understand him. He was taught to be seen and not heard. That probably accounted for so many bashful kids.

I'm sure those peers had no intention of being detrimental to their child's wellbeing. They were just so over-worked and deprived, they simply did not have time to analyze the situations at hand.

When a new baby arrived, if the proud new parents were too loving or showed the little one "too much" attention, some ole crab would come out with some of that good advice about "you'll spoil that baby before you know it," and if the baby cried very much for whatever reasons, "he was already spoiled rotten."

These poor little fellars heard "no-no" before they cut their teeth. That may be why so many of us have such negative attitudes. We all kinda feel like everything is a "no-no."

As soon as a child could walk and talk he was threatened with all kinds of "you're gonna get a spanking if you do that again" or "I'm gonna switch them legs if you don't stop that racket," or "I'll turn you over my apron and paddle your bottom," and then, with only a little more age, all of the above were implemented plus a few more impromptu punishments such as a slap across the face.

With a bunch of kids such as our household harbored, there was always a dispute going on, and often they erupted into a small scuffle, so our parents were really put to the test. They simply couldn't let us get by with everything, so we kept a trail hot going to the nearest peach tree. As our Mother put it, we were getting those "peach tree hickorys" (a saying for a small, limber branch for a switch).

It didn't take us little kids, who were subject to our Mother's discipline, very long to figure out if we got a small switch it wouldn't hurt as bad, plus we also learned if we'd start crying before she switched us she wouldn't "wear us out." A few times we'd half-way break the little limb before we handed it to her cause those didn't hurt at all. We just pretended they did.

Our Dad's punishment for the older boys was much more to be dreaded. He usually used that ole razor strap that hung on the back porch for any and all disciplining. Most of the time "his punishment exceeded the crime." I'm sure all he was thinking about was "sparing the rod and spoiling the child" and in his estimation a spoiled child was worse than the plague.

These cruel whippings were indeed carried out behind the woodshed, because my Mom would have intervened and called a halt about halfway through. One of the most dreaded punishments was getting a spanking at school and having to come home and report it to our parents. They immediately went into a rage and carted you off to the next room where they walloped the tar out of you when a good talking to would have served the purpose.

When we went visiting or shopping, and especially to church, we had to "toe the line" or suffer the consequences. We were not turned a loose to run and ramble around in someone else's house or shop. Most especially we knew not to misbehave during the worship services at church.

At church we got a lot of nudges and pinches from our Mom because we were too fidgety, but mostly because of our giggling. No matter how hard we tried we couldn't keep from giggling at something, whether it was an old toothless man with his mouth hanging open, or an old maid with too much white powder dusted on her face, with little round balls of rouge on her jaws, or the lady who stood up on the next row in front of us with her dress all stuck to her fanny, or someone's tummy growling; any and everything was funny and we couldn't stop laughing. Of course that misbehavior disrupted all of the people around us and we could see our Mom getting more and more exasperated. We'd put our hands over our mouths, hoping that would help, but it only enticed some other kid to get tickled.

Eventually our Mom leaned away over and promised to give us a good whipping when we got home. That worked and things weren't nearly as funny after that and she did keep her promise. It's a wonder we didn't .grow up hating to go to church, but we didn't; we mostly remembered the good times.

It was often thought that some of the younger men left home at an early age because of the cruel punishment they received at home for little or no reason.

In later years, the advice parents received about loving and tolerating their children was certainly a step in the right direction and the alternative methods of discipline were truly a blessing. But sometimes you wonder if we shouldn't have hung on to a little bit of that real disciplining that worked so well in years past.

'Looking After' Each Other

Being the large economy sized family that we were, we underwent all kinds of experiences, the greatest part of which were problems, often self-inflicted. We learned at an early age to fend for ourselves and look out for our own wellbeing; our parents tried to teach us to look out for each other, which was as it should have been but wasn't always the case. Having such varied personalities, we were often more interested in helping certain sisters or brothers who liked the same things we did.

As a whole our community was a close-knit one with everyone "looking after" each other in any way that was reasonable. If an interloper from out of town came around creating a disturbance or trying to pick a fight with one of our locals, everyone would come to his rescue with all kinds of verbal attacks, or, if need be, "first force" till the squabble was settled or the instigator of the disturbance left.

The older children in any family were handed the big responsibility of making sure the younger ones were safe and doing what their parents wanted them to do. There were always exceptions, and anyway, one overseer was not enough for nine to eleven self-willed kids of every awkward age and mentality.

Nearly always the kids with the most "far out" ideas were the ring-leaders. Things were boring enough without doing the same ole mundane rituals every day, so we were always looking for new ideas about easier ways to do our work or how to expand our horizons at playtime for more excitement.

There were also instances of looking out for ourselves first, such as the times when a younger one had some candy or good cookies and we could help him eat them to keep him from getting a tummy ache??? . . . or the times when a larger child was told to fill up the firewood box and he'd con the smaller ones into helping him, or when the older one was instructed to sweep the porch and he plotted a way to get a smaller one

135

to see how fast he could do it for the big reward of a hand clap when he finished.

Whenever there had been any kind of hanky panky, we'd all stick together and not tell on each other, for the purpose of not being told on when we were the guilty one. On several occasions we were very polite to pull out a chair for someone to sit on; of course we couldn't help it if the chair moved back a little too far just as they got ready to sit down. Even then we'd help them get up off the floor.

If we were chosen to go on a short trip or visit with our parents, we didn't even wiggle our forefinger at the others and say "giddy, giddy", for the simple reason that we wouldn't get to go either. Even at night we kept an ever watchful eye or ear for our siblings. When we heard a little fellar crawl off the bed and try to find a potty in the dark, we'd get up and help him. This, too, was prompted by an ulterior motive such as not wanting to sleep in a wet bed.

One little sister loved to "take care" so much that she brought some baby pigs in the house when it was cold and put them in a box by the fireplace. The little pigs just wanted to sleep with their mama, so they kept us all awake squealing and hopping out of their box, making it necessary for her to come to their rescue in the dark. She also liked to pet the little chickens and tried to dress them up, much to their disapproval.

We liked to tease her, since she had such a short fuse, to see how she'd react. It was always a surprise but she did react. On occasions our Mom wondered why she displayed such a temper. We didn't bother to admit we'd been aggravating her.

If we ran out of anything else to do we'd dress our little curly haired brother up in girls' clothes to see how cute he looked. At his age he didn't know the difference, and since he had only girls to play with, he probably thought he was one too.

While we were typically mischievous, small kids we were genuinely concerned about each other's well-being, especially if an injury or sickness was involved. We were very interested in trying to keep everyone well, since

136

we knew if one of us got sick it would spread till we had a house full of sick folks.

It must have been a great reassuring sight for our Mom to see two or three of us kids coming in from school in the rain with one coat spread over all those heads.

While playing in the yard or at school if someone fell out of a tree or stumbled over something, or got hit by something or someone and started crying, we'd all come running to see how badly he was hurt or help him up and try to console him.

At times it was hard to tell, but over the long haul we did "look after" each other, in one way or another.

Welcomed Hand-Me-Downs

When the older kids had hopelessly outgrown a garment it was assuredly handed down to the next smaller kid. If we liked the garment when it was new we were ever so glad to get them, but if we never cared for them in the first place we still didn't like them when they came down to us second-handed. Since we didn't have a choice, we wore them anyway; however, we weren't real careful with them, hoping something would happen to them so we'd be rid of them once and for all. Luckily or unluckily, as children, most of us had about the same measurements. No one was overly tall nor exceptionally plump, so there was no real cause for alterations on the garments except for maybe adding a bow or changing the belt to give them a little different appearance.

Occasionally a big flared skirt that one of my older sisters didn't like or couldn't get to hang just right when she put it on, got revamped and made into a dress for a smaller kid. All it needed was a little different colored material for a collar and maybe a little ric-rac here and there to make its new owner completely happy and to give my Mom the satisfaction of being able to salvage the skirt.

Many girls back then wore those real full skirted dresses that were often cut on the bias, and if you were sway-backed or pot-bellied, those poor old skirts drooped in the back or hiked up in the front and were not something to be proud of. We were indeed blessed not to have any of those extreme shapes. Some girls were even hump-backed because no one insisted they stand up straight nor carry themselves with a more attractive posture.

At some earlier time my Dad had bought my Mom a brown seal fur coat, and I loved the feel of the "luxurious" fur! After my Mom had outgrown it and it had rested several years in her wardrobe, she decided to cut it down and make me a coat out of it; nothing could have pleased me more! Other kids probably would not have worn it but I was enthralled with the idea of being the only one in my school with a fur coat (the fakes were not invented back then).

Another highlight in our lives that came about at least once a year was the visit from one of our aunts who always brought a big box of hand-me-downs in several kinds and colors. She had only one daughter, who worked and bought her own ready-made, store-bought clothes, and naturally, we thought they were far superior to ours.

We could hardly wait for this aunt to leave so we could start rambling around in those clothes to *see* what all she had brought. This w*as* the closest thing to Christmas we experienced. We were all on hand to dig in and check over all of that lovely garb. We tried on each and every item and stood in front of the mirror admiring ourselves at great lengths before letting anyone else try it on. this went on for hours as we tried on everything in the box, which included dress-up clothes, two-piece knitted suits, casual dresses and skirts, and even hats and gloves, which we had absolutely nothing appropriate to wear with; but that didn't hold us back. We strutted around on Saturday evening and Sundays with them on and felt like one of the Vanderbilts, while the other sisters anxiously awaited their turns to wear them later on.

One year a real live store-bought swimsuit had been included. We could hardly wait our turn to try it on and then to finally decide who it fit the best and who would be the first to wear it. T'was a terrible decision to have to make, since we all wanted it so desperately. It certainly looked funny to *see* one real swimsuit down at our wash hole! Everyone stared with envy at the "bathing beauty" who was wearing it. We were secretly hoping she'd soon outgrow it so we could get to wear it.

Some of the clothes that got handed down had been worn so much to school and church we were ashamed to wear them to those same places, so we tried real hard to rotate them around to wear on other occasions so as not to be embarrassed when everyone stared at us and started whispering to each other (always with their hands over their mouths and glancing over our way).

139

What few Sunday shoes we could afford were the only shoes that got handed down. Mostly we had one pair of all-purpose shoes at a time, and with everyday, all the time wear there was very little wear left in them to be handed down. We did save the remnants for picking blackberries, gathering brush brooms, and general field work. That always took care of them once and for all.

Gloves, capes, scarves and sweaters that didn't get lost or completely mutilated were definitely passed along to whoever could wear them or wanted them. We never wasted anything anyone could use because we couldn't afford to and I imagine we didn't want to. I find it hard to visualize growing up without "hand-me-downs!"

Necessary Mending

When I was young, ragged clothing was not the "in thing." No one went anywhere wearing clothing that had holes in them. It was really a disgrace to be seen away from home in "'holy" garments.

There were times when a hole would have looked better than the patches that some of us wore. Nonetheless, we wore them, along with most of our neighbors. In fact, some of the time our everyday garb had patches on top of patches.

If we snagged a new dress or pants or overalls, we simply could not afford to discard them, so our Mom labored tediously and consistently to try to recreate the weave or pattern of the garment that had been torn so we could get the expected wear out of it.

Ripped seams or pulled material didn't present much of a problem. They were just sewn back together on the sewing machine. If the fabric was sheer or of a loose weave, we'd have to double up a little extra material on the frayed side to cover the affected area. This usually left a puckered place on the one side and wasn't particularly attractive, but we wore it anyway.

The younger girls' sashes were constantly pulling out of the side seams, as this was the fastest way to catch, or halt a running child, and mending them was almost a full time job with all the little girls in our crowd. After several repair jobs, the sashes were considerably shorter on one side but was hardly noticed as we just sewed them right back in place time after time and went right along.

Buttons coming off and getting lost were always a problem. The men's shirts and pants, as well as the girls' clothes, were always needing a button or two. Our Mom had collected buttons for years and had an incredible collection of them, but you could very seldom find one that exactly matched the missing one.

After every washday some button would have to be replaced. We'd all sort through our collection and compare buttons till we came up with something close and try to use it in a less conspicuous place, trading buttons around till only the matching ones showed. Often we'd run out of matches so we just used what we had and felt self-conscious about the add-ons. There was little comfort in knowing ours didn't look any worse than our friends.

Most darned clothes might have looked bad but they felt all right, except for socks and stockings. Rayon hose was all we could afford and they took a lot of abuse being yanked up every few minutes. The socks for everyone were made of cotton and they never did fit worth a doodle. You spent a lot of time revamping them, plus your shoe heels rubbed them every step you took. As a result, little holes kept popping up. After every washday our Mom would get out her sewing box and find a needle she could thread and fumble around for her white thread so she could start darning some of the worst holes.

She really struggled to pull the fabric back together and make good strong stitches that would last several days. As a result, we would have a strong stiff ridge right down the middle of our heels and another that rubbed our big toes on the front. When we acquired a blister on our feet we never knew if the shoes caused it or our socks. It was also a very common sight to see the women with little sewed together ridges in their hose. Some of the time the thread used didn't match too good! No one ever entertained the idea of buying thread just for darning, we always used what we had on hand.

One of the hardest jobs that involved mending was taking apart a men's Sunday shirt collar and turning it over so the worn edges could not be seen. The stiff starch and constant hard rubbing on the washboard soon wore them out. They never did look quite right after they'd been turned over, and I'll bet they never felt the same either, but it had to be endured till we could do better.

Even though the mending of our clothes took a lot of our time, the mending was not confined to just our wearables. Sooner or later the sheets, pillow cases, bedspreads, dresser scarves, and any and everything else that could be repaired was mended in one way or another, hoping we could get just a little bit more wear or use out of them.

Making Soap From Scratch

I feel like our family was one of the greatest contributors to the success of the makers of Red Devil Lye or "potash," as we called it. We had to have used more homemade soap than anybody else anywhere. Our Mom was constantly yapping at us to build her a fire around our big black pot in the edge of the yard so she could boil up some more soap.

It was true that we had one of the world's largest families to dirty up clothes and floors and dishes and whatever else that had to be washed, but we still used a lot of soap per capita.

If there were laundry detergents on the market we either didn't know about them or we couldn't afford them; either way we never did buy any. All our washing aids were strictly home made at our home.

From one making to the next we saved all kinds of fatty meat scraps in a big lard pail to be used for that specific purpose. Our home grown hogs produced an abundance of fat and about one-fourth of it was dumped in that pail, along with skins from the side meat, the burned lard that had been used in cooking, the big bones with small meat scraps left on them, and any and all other fatty inedible scraps.

We had also saved an ample supply of wood ashes to be used with the above concoction to which was added a little water and Red Devil's Lye. When the meat pail got full of unusable fats, we mixed the right amount of ashes and water with it in the big black pot, started a good hot fire under it and set it all to boiling. It usually took a long time to cook it all together to be sure all the fat could be drained from the various sources but as soon as it was thought to be ready we'd strain all of the liquid out of that bundle of messy bones and skins, etc., and let it settle a while. Usually the next day we were off to the store to get another bottle of that Red Devil's Lye to add to the strained liquid to recook into some more of that all purpose soap.

144

The lye had to be handled with extreme caution as it was very potent and could eat a hole in your flesh in short order when it came in contact with it. Our Mom would not let us near the pot when she was putting together that mixture. On one occasion she got a tiny speck in her eye and even with a lot of cold water washing it left her eye very red and infected for months. She was very fortunate to have not lost her sight in that eye. I'm sure that was why she never let us near the opened cans.

When the fat, lye, ashes and water solution had boiled for the recommended time we'd let the fire die down and when it cooled some we'd put a top on the pot in case it rained before it solidified and got cold enough to remove from the pot. When it was cold we'd take our longest bladed butcher knife and cut all the way through it and remove a certain section which we'd chop up into small squarish pieces. As soon as it had all been removed we'd make preparations to store it in the smokehouse. We separated the pieces with paper or wood boards so it wouldn't stick together quite as bad, till we needed it.

It seemed like as soon as this batch was taken up we'd start saving up meat scraps and ashes for the next making. A real unending cycle, but there was an advantage to using this soap: we didn't need *any* bleaches and it sure cut down on the scrubbing time it took for the really dirty pieces on wash day, not to mention how effective it was in eradicating the dog greasy spots where the dogs slept on the porches.

145

Wash Day

Monday was the undisputed official wash day in our neck of the woods, weather permitting, and most of the time it did. It seemed like the Lord could see what a terrible batch of dirty clothes we'd accumulated all week and decided to let Monday be sunny or at least dry.

Since washing was such a big production and involved such a big area, we washed just once a week and even moved all the necessary equipment to our ever-dependable spring. This never-ending source of water was located at the bottom of a long steep hill situated in our cow pasture.

Early in the morning, immediately after breakfast, we'd strip off all the bed linens, gather up all the dirty clothes, towels, dish cloths, table covers and soiled dresser scarves or cushion covers, wad them all up in two or three sheets, tie a knot in the top, sling them over our backs, gather up the homemade soap, blueing (a bleach), starch, and assorted buckets and take off down the hill.

The wash tubs and pot (for boiling water and white clothes), along with the rub-boards, were left near the spring on some tables or benches that were built at just the right height to handle the job. Often the men carried the heavy dirty clothes down the hill and rounded up wood to burn under the big black pot full of water, but otherwise, the women folk did it all.

First off, one person would sort the colors, two or three others would fill the tubs with water. As soon as some water had warmed to add to the cold water in the tubs we'd start piling the dirty clothes in, white ones first. These always needed scrubbing on the rub boards with lye soap till all the dirty spots were removed. Some of them got boiled to remove stubborn grease spots and brighten them or remove all odors.

When piled in the pot of hot water a big stick stirred them around and was used to dip them up to be rinsed in the bluing water, wrung out, and hung out to dry.

146

Hanging them out to dry was not a simple thing; we hung them on the clothes lines, garden fences, and the rusty barbed-wire pasture fences. A couple of us were kept busy carrying and hanging the washed clothes. As soon as they were dry we'd take them down to make room for others. The rusty fences made iron rust spots on a lot of the white things and some of the clothes got snagged by the barbed wire, but we did the best we could with what we had to work with.

When all the white clothes had been washed, we'd start in on the next lightest colors, and so on till everything had been washed, including the men's super filthy overalls.

Then we'd empty up all the wash tubs and hang them up or turn them over to drain while we knocked over the black pot and left it upside down till the next week.

There were literally bushels of clean dry clothes that had to be transported up that long steep hill as we made our way homeward. As soon as they had been sorted, folded and piled up to be ironed we got busy doctoring our skinned knuckles, where we'd scrubbed the skin off on those harsh rub-boards.

We would have really dreaded these times except that it gave us girls some privacy to talk about our weekend dates or gossip about some of our neighbors and even confide our new knowledge about some of the guys we had dated or knew otherwise. At any rate, it was one of those facts of life and we just got on it and got it over with.

On some occasions our Mother would summon an old black lady to come and get the clothes to launder them. This was an old slave woman with no teeth, real pale eyes, bow-legs and winged feet that were seldom covered with shoes. Our Mother trusted her and often engaged her services. She always wore her head tied up as she came to gather up the clothes to be washed. She always gathered up a sheet full of clothes, tied them in a knot on top, hoisted them to the top of her head and took off down the road.

She'd leave our yard with a corncob pipe in her mouth, that big load on top of her head, and waddle off down the dusty road to her house. It was amusing to us to track her down the road cause she was so wing-footed. Anyone could identify her trail and often we would try to walk like that. Some of us were bow-legged too, but we were mostly pigeon-toed, so our walk was exactly opposite to hers.

There was seldom any cash involved for her services. She mostly wanted food or old clothes for her children and grandchildren, all of whom lived with her in her small house. A few times, several squares of soap went home with her without our approval, but I'm sure she thought she earned it.

Anyway, we always loved to see her and some of her family coming up to get the clothes. It sure meant an easier week for us.

Exciting Rolling Stores

One of the next best things to Santa Claus was the "Rolling Store." Whenever one pulled up in our yard, everyone came running from every direction to see what all was new and available. Some of us knew we could only look, as we had no money at all, so we just checked out everything and stood and gazed at the driver, who was a stranger.

As soon as the weird looking vehicle came to a stop we all gathered around as close as we could get as he climbed off his seat and started unlocking the back doors to give us a good look at all his wares. On some of these contraptions (trucks), little racks had been nailed on to the outside to hold the coops for the chickens which were used, largely, to pay for the merchandise.

Our Mom could hardly move for all the spectators and the smaller kids hanging on to her leg or dress tail. No one wanted to miss anything, but I'm sure she felt a sadness, looking at all those wistful faces who were going to be disappointed.

There was such a variety of items it took a long time to decide which ones we could afford. We nearly always needed a new oil cloth for our dining table and the 666 salve was almost all used up. The black shoe polish had been gone for weeks, and there was always a need for a card of white buttons. The banana flavoring was gone, and with hot weather coming up we needed a new can of talcum powder. Dad's shoe laces had been knotted so many times he could neither tighten nor loosen them, so we had to get some black shoe laces. My Mom always made cucumber pickles and she needed some alum and turmeric for those crunchy pickles. And, oh yes, we'd been owing Aunt Lizzie a letter for months cause our writing paper with lines had run out and we didn't have a single envelope in the house, those were also a must.

All these were "needed" items, but in addition to these must have items, he had all kinds of pretty things that we'd love to have. In her quandary for payment, our

Mom asked if she could trade in one of her hens and a dozen eggs. This, of course, was common procedure, so when she heard the affirmative reply she started scrounging around in her handbag to see how much money she could find, while one of the older girls checked out a vanity drawer for the change that was usually kept in there.

With everything summed up and estimates made on the needed household items, she sent us out to round up a certain old hen that had stopped laying. After much confusion and chasing, we came up with what looked like to us was the right one; since they were all Domineckers it was hard to tell one from the other. It happened we had caught the wrong chicken, so we had to start the chase all over again with Mom leading the way and pointing out the exact hen.

Eventually we had nabbed the right chicken, fetched a dozen eggs and at long last were ready to negotiate the deal. When all the "musts" had been taken care of, there was a little extra money left over which my Mom figured she could spend on some pretty bright colored material to trim some dresses with and much to our surprise and joy, some of those chocolate drops which we had been drooling over ever since the glass jar was uncovered.

When the little truck driver's patience and Mom's money had all run out, the little man began packing up all his assorted goods getting ready to head off down the road. Just before he slammed the doors shut he took a quick look around to make sure he hadn't added one of the kids to his inventory.

He had actually been there for so long our chickens had set up housekeeping under the modified truck. My Mom noticed them and started shooing them out from under there, as the dogs came running up barking to see what all the noise was about.

The completely exhausted driver climbed up in his seat after he had cranked the ole "flivver" and tried to get "her" backed up. Much to everyone's dismay he had a flat tire. The poor ole threadbare tires just wouldn't hold air.

He climbed down from his perch, rounded up a jack, raised the old contraption up a few inches, pumped up the tire and hurriedly cranked on the old jalopy till it fired up again.

In his mad frenzy to get going he had stepped in some fresh chicken litter, which irritated him even more as he hopped to the side of the yard to scrape most of it off.

He was really exasperated as he yanked his old truck around, trying desperately to make an escape before something else happened. I don't remember any of the drivers' names, as if there were any introductions. I rather suspect they had a rapid turnover in that department and I firmly believe they were all descendants of "Job," but we sure looked forward to their visits.

Making Syrup
For Better Or Worse

In some instances Fall was considered to be a winding down time, but as I recall, it was a re-winding time. Along with gathering corn and picking cotton and school starting there was this activity called making syrup to contend with.

The syrup referred to here was formally known as sorghum. You were definitely not set for cold weather unless you had an ample supply of sorghum. This "necessity" was made from a special syrup cane that all the farmers planted, mostly for their own use. When the cane stalks put on a large seeded head and its leaves turned a different color, it was time to strip the leaves, cut off the heads, cut down the stalks, stack them and haul them by mule and wagon to the community syrup cooker, who had reserved this special time for processing your crop.

You could smell the sweet, slightly stinky odor a long time before you got to the syrup mill, or designated place. In spite of the heat, the bees and every other uncomfortable thing you could imagine, we just had to go watch the process.

First thing was feeding the cane stalks into the grinding mill, which was turned by a mule that went round and round, making the grinder squeeze the sticky juice from the stalks. When the container under the grinder was full, it was emptied into one of the large copper trays over intense heat to start the syrup making process.

All the kids had to taste the freshly squeezed juice before it was heated. It wasn't very good to me. I preferred to cut a joint of the cane, peel it, slice off a small chunk and chew it. This was a slow process, since the small bites had very little juice and the pulp had to be spit out. But it tasted better that way and gave us something to do while we waited for the finished product.

The first big tray boiled up a greenish, nasty looking foam that was skimmed off and tossed into a big gooey looking bucket and saved for the hogs. (They got everything we couldn't eat). As soon as this first vat was suitably skimmed off and boiled, the mixture was switched over to a second big tray. Here it continued to cook to a certain stage and then moved over to the third and final vat. When it was relatively thick and transparent the maestro announced it was ready to be poured up into permanent containers.

Occasionally a bee (or two) would lose its bearings and fall into the super hot goo. As soon as they were noticed by the cook he'd scoop them up and plop them over into the slop bucket. It didn't make any difference to us, 'cause that syrup must have been 700 degrees F, and it was definitely sterilized. Anyway, we were more than glad to get rid of a few bees and hoped some other such mishap would befall the others. We spent the whole time batting and dodging them, and their tempers were really stirred up by the time the cooking was over.

Some years we'd wind up with several gallons of syrup and some years we'd have only a few. Regardless, the syrup maker got his portion of whatever we had for his pay.

Everybody looked forward to sampling the new syrup with hot biscuits and butter. It was a tradition at our house to pour the sorghum on our plate, cut off some butter and add to it and stir and smash it all up till it was well blended, then take a buttered biscuit and sop it up. This went on and on, as we gorged ourselves, trying to make the syrup and biscuits come out even. Most mornings, our breakfast wasn't complete without it.

If there were biscuits left from breakfast and we were there all day, we's bore a hole in the side of the cold biscuit, pour sorghum in it and eat that for an in-between meal snack. This was rather messy but it cured our hunger, at least temporarily. Another frequent use for this syrup was candy with peanuts, a big favorite in our neck of the woods. Our grandmother made super gingerbread and gingersnaps with sorghum. One thing it wasn't suitable for was as a sweetener. It had a horrible taste in tea or coffee.

By early spring of the next year most of our syrup supply was exhausted, so we'd go to the original source, the sorghum maker, and purchase some of his stockpile. If his was also depleted we'd have to resort to our home-canned jellies and preserves till the next fall when, God willing, we'd have fresh supply.

Road Scrape Spectacle

All of the roads in our area were dirt roads. Some of them were sandy and passable in all kinds of weather, while some of the others were powdery and dusty, but a few of them were red clay - like earth which mired easily in wet weather and created a great deal of havoc as a lot of cars got stuck on them or slid into a ditch. Luckily though the traffic was no problem, as there was only one car on the road at a time.

By and large, the roads were well kept with the ditches on either side relatively clean to carry the excessive rain water off. If there were continuous heavy rains in the winter or early spring, the most traveled roads would develop deep ruts which made for rough bumpy riding. The drivers would make every effort to straddle the deepest ruts wobbling from one side of the road to the other trying to avoid them, but sometimes there was no way. These "fair weather" roads just had to be endured in the rainy months till the weather "opened up."

When drier weather came the heavy wide road scrapes were sent out from the county seat in every direction to smooth up the road surfaces one more time. These huge, rough looking contraptions were man-handled by prisoners or "convicts" as we called them, dressed in black and white striped uniforms, supervised by guards who carried double-barreled shotguns wherever they went.

These wide scrapes were horse-drawn with large, strong horses pulling them. There were six horses pulling at one time, and that was quite a show!

As the scrapes came rumbling down the road, kicking up a big cloud of dust, all the local residents dropped what they were doing and came running out in their yards to see them and watch those unusual performances; as they dreaded the extra housework that was sure to follow. It sure didn't take long for all that dust to come

155

billowing through those open doors and windows to settle all over the furniture.

The driver was busy holding all those reins and enjoying the attention, so it was necessary for an extra person to walk along beside him to crack that long skinny whip to keep the horses moving in the right direction. He knew he was the center of attention so he threw in several extra whacks to show off his expertise. The noise that whip made could be heard a whole mile. That ole guy cracking that whip would have put "Lash LaRue" to shame! I'm sure most of the whip-cracking was unnecessary but the more he snapped it the better we liked it. We could hardly get our work done with all that excitement around.

The driver was instructed by the guard to stop at certain places around noon and at night. He needed a lot of space to park the scrape and un-hitch and feed the horses. A watering place was also necessary. Fortunately, we had such a place near our family cemetery, which was situated alongside the road, and we were delighted to be given such a privilege.

Our Dad would go with us to where they were feeding the horses so we could inspect the whole operation, while he chatted with the guard. We would have loved for the whip-cracker to give us a demonstration, but the horses were trained to react to that sound so that was out of the question. He did let us handle the whip and see how long and strong and narrow it was and see how the handle was put on.

All of this knowledge made us feel superior for days! We couldn't wait to see some of our friends and tell them about it. We could just see the envy in their eyes as they listened so intently.

As soon as their lunch hour was over and the horses had been watered, the convicts started hitching up the horses and getting in gear to move on down the road yelling and rattling and kicking up a lot more dust. If we were not overly busy with our work, we'd run along behind the scrape on that smooth soil till they were out of sight.

That soothing feeling under our bare feet was sheer ecstasy.

Occasionally, the whole company would turn back several miles down the road as nightfall approached and come back to leave their scrape and horses at this same place overnight. That was a very great unexpected pleasure. We could listen to the big horses stomping around and snorting all night, plus, we could be right there early the next morning with or without breakfast, to see them get hitched up as soon as a truck brought the guard and the convicts back.

In the meantime, everyone in the community hoped and prayed it wouldn't rain till the dirt was all packed down and settled so they wouldn't get stuck nor track muddy shoes all over the house.

Churning

It certainly was nice when we didn't have enough milk from one day to the next to have to churn (according to us kids). We did miss the butter, but sometimes we could get butter from one of our neighbors, 'cause her folks "didn't eat much of it."

Every family had milk cows and kept a tall pottery type churn sitting around with milk in it. The tops were always covered with a white cloth tied around it. The object of the churn with milk was hoping the milk would clabber (congeal), with the cream content coming to the top, leaving all the clabbered milk below. At this stage it had to be churned and churned and churned till the butter collected in a lump and could be scooped up by hand.

Our whole family loved buttermilk (when it didn't taste like bitter weed or wild onions), which happened especially in the spring when the pasture was (some years) full of the stuff. When that happened the hogs got all the buttermilk except what we needed to make bread. In cold weather the churn was kept near or on the hearth so the warmth would speed up the clabbering process. In warm or hot weather there was no problem, except you could smell the soured milk when you got near the churn.

We were always leery of the cats which were always cuddling up real close to the churn. We were afraid they'd try to crawl up on it or knock it over. Some of us were kept busy scatting the cats away. If our mother had time she'd sit and churn and eat, or read and rock for hours and seemed to enjoy the rest. But at other times, us kids rotated around taking turns after much parental coaxing.

It seemed like every other day was my turn and I hated it with a passion. There was no way I could dash that dasher and color or draw; the very best I could do was to sing or make up a poem or read a little and daydream, always envying the other kids who were playing. After swapping hands and complaining for what seemed like hours never missing a beat, I'd finally get through. No one, but no one, ever thought I *enjoyed* that job.

The only switching I ever remember getting was a lick or two from my Dad, who got tired of my procrastinating about getting started with my churning.

I don't remember how everyone else passed their time away during that dreaded job, but they weren't nearly as vocal about their displeasure with it as I was.

In a lot of cases, if the churning had been going on for hours, our Mom would add a little warm water to it to try to hasten the butter's "coming." Some of the time we'd peep under the lid to see if there were lumps or specks of butter on top. If we could see either, we'd yell out good and loud, "The butter's come." At this time our Mother, knowing not to take our word for it, would come and check it out. She'd take the dasher and try to push all the butter together. If it didn't stick together she'd make us churn a little longer.

One of the worst things about churning was the little spatters of milk that landed on everything around, especially on Mom's glasses. It took a long time to find and wipe off all those little spatters when we finally finished churning.

Those dashers were about 2½ feet long round sticks with crossed pieces of thick wood on one end. The top of the churn was a round, perfectly fitted piece of one-inch thick wood with a smooth round hole in the middle that was a little larger than the dash. The movements for banging the butter out of the milk were up and down till you practically flopped over from exhaustion or bumped your arm out of joint!

When the butter finally "came" our Mom would cram her clean hand, with her sleeves rolled up over her elbow, down into the churn and gather the butter loosely in her hand and dump it in cool water to be washed, salted and shaped in a wooden mold. It was then stored in our cupboard to be used for spreading, seasoning, and cooking.

It sure disappeared in a hurry to be so slow a "coming" and there was that dreaded procedure to endure the next or the next day. Eventually we got a contraption called a "Daisy Churn" and this was a little bit easier, or at least different to use. It was a large, squarish metal container with a wheel on the side. It was easier to turn it, but the time for churning was about the same. The biggest difference was the Daisy Churn was bigger and harder to clean, so it was really hard to tell if it was an improvement.

I'm sure there was rejoicing in the camp when the churning era came to an end.

Easter In The Country

Being kids, in our minds Easter was synonymous with a bright sunshiny, warm day. We had vivid ideas about the Marys (of the Bible), finding an empty tomb just as dawn broke through and that Jesus, being the light of the world, had certainly risen up with the beautiful bright sunlight. It also meant we could put on our new Sunday spring dresses to go to church.

If our Mom had made us thin cool dresses, the weather was sub-zero, on the other hand, if she had made warm, long-sleeved dresses, the weather was the warmest on record for that day. Since we only wore these clothes for such a short time, it didn't really matter that much; just as soon as we got home from church, we had to change our clothes so we'd be ready to hide and hunt eggs.

Our schools did not enjoy a spring break, but we did have an Easter egg hunt on Friday before Easter. We also had an Easter program, of a sort, that morning. If an older child had consented to learn and recite a poem, we listened to that and the Easter story as depicted in the Bible. I can imagine all of the Bible verses on this day that answered the roll call were directly connected to "Christ arose."

When and if dogwoods had begun to bloom we'd have a big bouquet of those, and our teacher explained the correlation of these blossoms and the dogwood tree to the crucifixion. We kinda went all-out for Easter, especially if the weather cooperated.

In preparation for the many egg hunts we saved all our eggs and borrowed some from Granny so we could color them to our best ability for hiding and hunting and finally eating. We searched high and low for all the broken and almost used up crayons we could find, boiled the eggs till they were well done, cooled them a little in water, dried them off and "lit" into coloring all kinds of shapes and designs all over them.

161

We didn't use the good gumption of making them a brilliant solid color, we fouled them all up with weird patterns and terrible color combinations. This project kept us engrossed for hours. Our concentration was so intense we'd forget to squabble and scuffle with each other. As soon as we had them all painted up we'd do a little "practice run" with them to see how good they looked all hidden away. It was always hard to decide who would be the first to hide them. This settlement was often made by drawing straws.

The pastures were the only places we had grass growing, so we'd skinny under the barbed wire fences to find a place where the grass was tallest and hope we didn't step on any of them after they were hidden, nor any of the other unpleasant things in the pasture.

The big kids always took advantage of the little ones and hid the eggs in holes where they could be covered up real good or placed them up on a tree limb out of reach and out of view, making it hard for us to find them all. We very seldom got them all rounded up without smashing at least one of them. As we grew hungry, we'd sample a few of them, making it necessary to boil a few additional ones to keep the supply up.

A lot of times the colors had bled through the warm eggshells, making the whites inedible, so we just ate the yellows which were bluish green from overcooking.

When we finally got them to school the teacher would bring out the brightly colored candy eggs she had bought and they were all mixed up together. We were much more eager to find those candy eggs even though they became awfully sticky from over-handling. (They were not wrapped like the ones you see today).

The only places we had to hide them on the school grounds were behind little clumps of weeds or sticks, or behind a tree root or up in the little bushes nearby. All of the school yards were sandy areas with no grass on them, so it took some ingenuity to find places to hide all those eggs in the allotted time.

When the "all clear" signal had been given there was a major stampede with big kids rushing out the doors shoving the little kids aside with as many as three kids grabbing for the same eggs. Several kids tripped over each other and even over their own feet trying desperately to be the one with the most eggs. The one with the most eggs got the cherished prize which was in most cases a very inexpensive toy but very much appreciated, as toys were so rare.

After about three re-hidings of those battered and sticky eggs the hunt was considered over and the teacher took them all up and passed them around so that all the kids would get some. We immediately started cracking them on our knees or on the other fellow's head, peeling them and eating the ones which looked good enough. We mostly ate the colored sugary coating off the candy eggs and threw the other parts away.

Of course we were about half sick when we arrived home and couldn't eat any supper, but by the next day (Saturday) we were all set to go visiting so we could play hiding eggs again.

Building Them Barbed Wire Fences

A farm wasn't a farm without a cow and mule, which always required a barbed wire fence to keep them at home. Even with the fences, they'd often stray off to the next man's pasture or go trotting off down the road. To erect a good, decent pasture fence you had to have a lot of posts;, a lot of wire, one or two sets of post hole diggers, and most of all, a lot of hard work.

First, each farmer gave a lot of thought to just what all he wanted to fence in. He had to consider the fertility of the soil, always saving the best and most level land for his crops, patches, and gardens. Then he'd make sure he wasn't enclosing any of his neighbor's land.

He checked out the proposed line for fences to see how rocky it was. Some of the land was so rocky a good post hole could not be dug in it, so all efforts were made to avoid these areas. Having mastered this engineering feat he set about finding some suitable posts of locust, red oak, or chestnut oak because they would withstand the weather better. Then, of course, the trees had to be cut down and cut into suitable lengths. If by any chance he didn't have appropriate trees on his own farm he'd set about trying to con his neighbor out of some that were on his farm. Sometimes this involved swapping trees or work to each man's satisfaction.

Next on the agenda was digging the post holes. This was a long and hard, physically exhausting, procedure that went on and on. Often the ground was hard and each hole had to be about a foot deep so as to hold the posts erect during inclement weather and to withstand the nailing on of the wire.

The holes had to be dug approximately eight to ten feet apart and when you're talking about fencing in several acres, that's a lot of post holes. The poor ole farmers and their older sons would work and sweat and slave as long as they could hold out; their hands would become blistered and peeled all over on the insides. The worn gloves that were used to handle the wire was only partial protection, and it wasn't long till you heard someone yell out, "Doggone it!" and start flinging his hand. He had been stuck or scratched and had to find something to doctor it with. These scratches made deep sores that always got infected and had to be doctored with all the home remedies anyone knew about before they finally healed up.

When all the posts had been put in place and tamped with soil and small rocks, the big rolls of barbed wire were brought in to be nailed to them. It was an awful chore to handle those super sharp barbs on those large, heavy rolls of wire. Mostly they were rolled on the ground and unraveled from there as much as possible. A big supply of sharp-ended staples had been bought to hammer over the wire onto the posts. These nails were carried either in a big overall jumper (Jacket) or in a carpenter's apron, which had a big front pocket. These places were easier to get to and heavens knows you needed all the help you could get.

At least two people had to man this operation, and if others were available, it made the job a lot faster. At best, this work went on for days. Four or five strands of wire had to be placed on each post. The lowest one had to be low enough to keep the calves or goats and sheep from crawling under. Not many people had sheep or goats, but occasionally someone would raise a few and they would cohabit with the other animals in the same fenced in pasture.

When finished, these pastures with cattle grazing created a peaceful, homey look for us all. The drawbacks were the fences blocked our shortcuts to the neighbors' houses or the store. It wasn't long till we mastered the art of climbing up on the wire to the top of the fence and jumping down or pulling up the wire to open up a space wide enough for us to crawl through. This was the biggest contributor to our snagged dress tails or sweaters, but we weren't going all around that darn pasture to get where we needed to go, if there was any other way.

165

If our Dad happened to be watching we just marched around that fence like little soldiers, never once thinking about climbing on that plagued fence. He always seemed more concerned about preserving his fence than our walk-worn legs.

It seemed like the fences had hardly been finished till the ole cows would poke their heads through to test the grass that was always greener on the other side. This constant shoving on the strands loosened them up considerably; you couldn't walk around those fences many steps before you spotted wads of cow or mule hair on those sharp twisted barbs.

To keep the cows and mules from getting out, we'd have to walk all around the pasture fences at intervals to make sure the strands of wire were intact and the posts upright. We often took a hammer and nails with us just in case we found a problem. When we found one, it took us all to hammer a nail in the right place, giving our best efforts to the cause. Even then, a few of us wound up with smashed thumbs.

This took a lot of our valuable play time, so to keep our minds off our job we'd often brush up on our whistling. Only a few of us could stick two fingers in our mouth and whistle good and loud, but all of us could do a make-shift whistle through our bottom teeth. It didn't sound like much, but it helped us pass the time that wound up being two or three hours long.

Making A Vegetable Garden

Our garden was in the same place always, mainly because we had to have a tall fence around it to keep the chickens out. We always had a couple of hungry dogs running around in the yard so we didn't worry about the rabbits eating the vegetables. The fence even kept the terrapins and frogs out. The only devourers other than ourselves were the birds.

Each year our mom saved the very best of each vegetable, removed their seeds, dried and saved them for the next year's planting. These best seeds, after being dried thoroughly, were wadded up in paper and stored in little glass jars to keep the dampness and bugs out till early the next spring.

In preparation for the spring planting, we had to rake off all the dead vines and bushes and burn them so our Dad could bring the plow through the gate to plow up the ground horizontally and vertically, pulverizing the ground. Then he'd change plows and layoff rows equal distance apart and leave the garden to be fertilized and planted by our Mom and a kid or two.

At this time, our Mom recruited the lot of us, rounded us up some ole discarded pails and/or pans, a hoe and a shovel, and led us into the chicken house. Under the board racks where the chickens roosted were little mounds of droppings, which was supposed to be super fertilizer for the garden and flowers. So we started scraping and shoveling it up into our containers and carried it to the designated rows in the garden. As soon as this supply was exhausted we'd move off down to the barn into the cow stables. This was a dreaded procedure because this manure was quite smelly and often damp. Under our Mother's supervision and insistence we cleaned out that area too and took load after load to the garden to put into its appropriate place.

Having dumped all of that manure, along with a little commercial fertilizer, on the rows we'd be supervised in dropping the precious seeds at just the right distance and in just the right amounts in those rows. As soon as we'd seeded two or three rows someone would start covering them up and packing the soil. We all liked this part cause the loose dirt felt good on our bare feet.

This whole procedure was carried out according to the "signs," the signs being either illustrated in the almanac or explained orally by the neighbors, or grandparents, who had received the knowledge from their forefathers. These signs had to be adhered to the letter. No substitutions or delays, as this would lead to a poor crop, or maybe all vines with no food on them.

Some things were planted at different times with as much as two weeks in between, so it kept my father busy referring to his calendar to be sure he was planting everything at just the right time. As soon as one or two groups of seeds had been planted, another bunch was in line to be planted, till all the garden space had been used up. If a nice April shower came along at just the right time, the little seeds would sprout in a few days, but in spite of our best efforts an occasional chicken would scramble under the wire fence and start scratching left and right tearing up the new plants before we ever noticed them. It was necessary to keep an eye out for those destructive hungry critters at all times. Every precaution we knew about was taken to keep the bugs and worms off the plants. Things like soapy water, snuff, tobacco juice, etc., were used and if anyone came up with a new preventive measure we used that too.

The green beans and "Irish" potatoes usually attracted the most bugs. We were kept busy inspecting the leaves for bugs and eggs. A lot of eggs were laid in little patches, so we'd smash them in big quantities. The wormy looking potato bugs we knocked on the ground and stepped on them, the little lady bugs were easy to catch and kill, but they seemed to appear from nowhere and were hard to keep killed.

The business of keeping the plants hoed around and weeded went on forever. It got to be such a hassle that one of my sisters would develop what we called a "hoe sickness." Actually we were all worn out with hoeing everything everywhere, but our parents were relentless. We were forced to keep on keeping on.

Even with all the drawbacks the plants usually got grown and produced *some* food for eating and canning, as well as some to share with neighbors whose gardens had not yet come in.

When the green bean plants began to put out runners, my brothers would gather tall canes and stick them in the ground at each plant all the way down each row, then they'd get strings and tie four of them together across two rows, making them look like teepees. We younger kids thought that was a new playground and ran through them from one end to the other trying to catch each other. That was very entertaining for several days till something different came along.

Along the edge of our garden, next to the fence, was where the asparagus, Jerusalem artichokes, dill, and strawberries were planted. We were constantly sneaking through the garden to check out the turning strawberries; we liked them better just before they got ripe. Our poor Mom always wondered why we never had any more strawberries. Ours were not the ever bearing variety, so they were soon out of season anyway.

When the vegetables were mature enough to gather, we'd pick them or dig them and sit outside in the swing to string beans or shell limas and peas. We enjoyed doing that, but peeling tomatoes to can, or digging potatoes, or shucking and silking corn had to be done standing; it was also a lot messier. The very worst never-ending job was canning vegetable soup mix. It went on and on. Freezers were completely unknown at that time, so everything was canned. The hot fires in the stove for heating the water in the canners and boiling the lids and rubber jar rings made the temperature soar, especially having to boil the jars of prepared vegetables for long lengths of time to make sure the jars were sealed and that such non-acid vegetables like green beans were fully processed.

Fortunately, most of the time, by late summer the gardens were pretty bare except for the sweet potatoes, a little okra, a few peas, and the very young turnip greens.

Then, just as in years past, we'd go around and gather those select seeds left to dry on the vines and stalks to shell and preserve for the next year's planting.

Summer Storms

Since time began, weather has been the most talked about subject, and our area was no exception. Just as soon as you greeted your neighbor with a "Howdy do" or "Good Mornin," you immediately broke in with a comment about the weather: "how hot it is," "how nippy the air has got," "how much we need a shower," or "how wet it is" if it had rained for several days, along with many "'clouds" as how the dirt needed wringing out and how much they'd like to see a few days of bright sunshine.

Since this was farming territory, the weather really controlled all of the outside activities. As kids, we didn't recognize the significance placed on it, but as we grew older and were able to accept more of the responsibilities we did comprehend the reasons for that enormous interest in the weather.

If the ground was too dry it was too hard to plow, if it was too wet, it could neither be plowed nor hoed. If it was unseasonably cold, there was no need to plant the seeds, they wouldn't germinate, plus you'd get sick if you stayed out too long and the animals didn't perform as well. If it was too hot, everything would wilt, including farmers, plants, and animals, often resulting in a poor crop.

In the early spring when the crops and gardens had been planted, we often wished and even prayed for it to rain so the seeds would sprout and we could get an early start with the plants. The April showers were normal and most of the planting was centered around them. At this time of year, these instant showers were called "April showers." During this time there'd hardly be any clouds around when suddenly big drops of rain would start peppering down almost instantly, often before we could take cover. When we got wet from one of these sudden downpours our parents would blurt out, "Haven't you got sense enough to get in out of a shower of rain?"

Usually when we could see a sizable cloud approaching, our Dad (the weather vane) would watch closely as the formations and colors changed, all the while keeping check on the wind velocity and any signs of lightning, so he could unhitch the mules and send us home before the storm reached us.

The few times we'd get caught in a downpour, we enjoyed it! It felt so good being cooled off and wet all over. We didn't think about the possibility of being hit by lightning until we heard of a nearby farmer or mule being struck by it. Often we'd stand under a tree for shelter, waiting for the rain to slack up. As we stood there we'd giggle about how we looked with that wet garb glued to us. When we'd loosen the cloth up in one spot, it got tighter somewhere else, which made for even more giggling our poor ole straw hats sure drooped as soon as they got good and wet. The way we restored them was to place the brims stretched and straightened out on a flat surface, often held down with little rocks. At intervals, we'd have to punch the crowns up with our fists or stuff wadded up paper in them. After a day or so they were dried and ready to wear again. They didn't feel quite the same at first, but after a day or two's wearing them they were back to normal.

When the weather got unbearably hot and the humidity very high, we were sure to have an electric storm before we got any relief from the heat. Our thunderstorms seemed to come at night, at which time our Mother was almost uncontrollably frightened.

As soon as one approached she'd roll out of bed and start pacing the floor, pretending to be lowering the windows or closing the shutters on the porches. It was powerfully hot in those bedrooms with the windows closed; luckily, we could leave the doors open, since there were covered porches around them.

If the wind was severe our Mother would close those doors and start wringing her hands full time. She'd trot from one window to the other, looking out and jumping back when the lightning flashed and a loud clap of thunder followed.

We kids stayed in the bed with our heads covered up most of the time, but we became uneasy with those loud claps of thunder and howling winds which really bent the trees with their intensity.

Our poor grandma had a tin roof on her house and we could recall hearing the hailstones banging on it as though they would come through, when spending the night and we'd have severe storms in the hot weather. At least our house had a taller roof that was covered with shingles, which muffled a lot of the sound.

Our biggest worry was our Mom's getting so excited. As soon as the wind and lightning subsided she'd settle down and go back to bed at which time we could all unwind and go back to sleep, most of the time proud of the rain that was so badly needed by us and the crops.

We couldn't survive without the rains, but a lot of the time we dreaded the storms, especially if they brought much hail to tear up the young plants and flowers. There were several weeks of dry weather during "laying by" times, and then we'd be lambasted with "Dog Day showers," which were exactly like the "April showers," but came later in the summer when we were trying to gather the crops.

In short, everything that could be blamed on the weather was, since no one could control it and no one person had to shoulder responsibility for it.

Readying A Barbecue

Everyone in our community seemed to be completely obsessed with barbecue. The only kind we were familiar with was a young pig home-grilled over hot hickory and oak coals and basted endlessly with a very hot vinegar and pepper sauce seasoned with salt, pepper, and butter.

If you didn't have much patience, you didn't mess with this delicacy. It took hours to roast it just right. Preparations were made well in advance and plans worked out for someone to watch this young pig cook from the wee hours of the morning, like 2:00 a.m., till late lunch time. A proper pit was dug and a fire had been built nearby to burn down the green hickory and oak wood so that the coals could be piled in the pit prior to placing and securing a heavy wire rack on which the pig was to be grilled.

These coals had to be cooled down to a smoldering stage that produced very little smoke before the slaughtered and dressed pig could be placed on the rack. If there were rotisserie style cookers on the market back then we never saw any; therefore, the meat (a whole pig, minus head, innards, and fat) had to be turned frequently, the hard way, by more than one person.

Since the turning presented such a problem, the coals had to be ashy grey so as not to burn the meat on that side before it could be turned. Each time the pig was turned it had to be basted in order to acquire that sourish, pungent taste that made the meat so delectable.

The older brothers were unanimously elected to do the barbecue, so they took turns with the cooking. They'd put an old quilt on the ground fairly close to the barbecue pit and catch a few winks in between the turning and basting episodes. The old hound dogs were about the only company they had at this hour. They stood around as close as they could get without getting burned, lapping their chops and wishing there was a way they could get at that meat.

174

Occasionally an old hoot owl would voice its disapproval at someone disturbing its peace, or a few bats would swoop down trying to figure out what was going on at that time of night. Before the usual wake-up time the roosters would wake up and decide to awaken everyone else with their loud noisy crowing, after which all kinds of songbirds would start chirping and screeching and whistling and mocking each other.

After all these disturbances a relief cook would show up, since he couldn't sleep anyway and start piling some more logs on the fire to make more coals to add to the pit. Before the night watchman left, they'd hassle around turning the pig and adding more sauce to the carcass. No one was in favor of shortcuts for fear of ruining the flavor, so there were no other methods considered.

By this time, our Mom and Dad would be up boiling and stewing chicken, beef, squirrel, and maybe a few doves and turtle to be ground up for that other great treat that had to be served with the barbecue, none other than that infamous Brunswick stew!

We'd eat a scanty breakfast to the smell of all that half-cooked meat which we could smell all over the place. As soon as we'd finished breakfast and washed up all those dishes, we'd have to start peeling tomatoes, potatoes, and onions to be added to all that deboned meat which was ground up and seasoned to be cooked an hour or so longer, while we prepared a dozen or more dishes for the crowd we expected to feed.

We didn't go to all this trouble just for our own family, we invited our best friends or hunting buddies or card-playing friends or closest neighbors to come and eat dinner with us. They never refused. I think they could smell those delicious aromas all over the neighborhood and weren't about to turn down an invitation to eat something so special and hard to prepare.

These feasts were all eaten outside. Big granite slab tables had been built for this purpose and this is where all the barbecuing and other big "feed bags" took place.

For this event we'd always make gobs of that good ole "Tetley Tea" and even get some store-bought white loaf bread to eat with the stew. The traditional way to eat the stew was spread over a slice of that white bread. 'Twas indeed a real treat and most of the time scrumptious if it were made by the old master stew-makers who never missed.

When the barbecue was sampled all around and judged to be done, the browned pig was moved by sections to a meat table where at least two people started instantly chopping it up into little pieces. As soon as a big pan was filled and spread with some more of that special sauce another section of pig would be taken up and cut into little pieces. The really brown crisp skin was delicious and several people would stand around waiting to get a taste of it before dinner was served.

Eventually the invited crowds would come straggling up and the blessing would be asked after which some of us would make a mad dive to get into that stew and "cue." We often ate so much of the rich greasy stuff we'd be sick at our stomach. If it hadn't been for a bunch of sour pickles and gallons of ice cold tea, we wouldn't have survived.

Most of us kept eating as long as it tasted good whether we'd had our fill or not. A lot of the time there was an abundance of the meat and stew left so we'd measure up quarts or pints and give it to the guests to take home with them. We had no way of keeping it for very long before it spoiled, since there were no real refrigerators nor freezers to store it in.

The cooks were the heroes of this day. Almost no one ate that feast without paying their compliments to those cooks, and rightly so. After all, they had spent two days preparing for it and lost a whole night's sleep cooking it just for those moments of praise.

The Community Blacksmith

Every community in our farming county had a blacksmith. He may not have been topnotch, but he would tackle shoeing a mule and sharpening plows with a lot of energy and velocity. These were two of the most needed services on the farm.

Because of the ever-present smoke and dirty coal piles, these men had their shops a little way from their homes. If they were conscientious workers and produced good work their reputations would spread to other communities and often a good half of his work was for people in other areas and for very little, if any, pay.

In his shed or shop, was a coal bin and open fireplace, called a forge, with a bellows, which was used to get quick air to the fire and produce a hotter blaze faster. Usually, hanging on a big nail, was where he kept his cruddy leather apron which afforded some protection from some of the hot sharp tools or mules' hooves.

Coal was always used to produce the needed heat and that, of course, had to be purchased at the nearest market. The blacksmith usually went to the coal yards with a couple of "tow sacks" to scrape up small pieces of coal and even the coal dust, to be used for his fires, because it was cheaper, and heaven knows he needed all the breaks he could get to compensate for all his free labor, plus the coal didn't last very long at best with all the trifling small jobs he had to do.

In the forge he had to burn the coal to a bright red so as to heat the metal he had to work with to a pliable texture. He kept a couple of large anvils, some lifting tongs and a couple of heavy metal hammers with which to pound the heated metal objects to the desired shapes. He had to wear long leather gloves for all of these heated metal tasks to prevent his hands and arms from being scorched by the heat from the hot coals.

Needless to say, this job required a strong man who could endure the heat and cope with the strain of holding the work animals the proper way to either put new horseshoes on or put extra nails and repair the ones they already had. Putting on new shoes required the mule's hooves to be trimmed before they could be nailed on smoothly and evenly.

It took a lot of experience to know how to put those nails in the right place and at the right depth, along with securing them as he went. Before this tortuous task commenced the blacksmith would render his "nose-twisting" treatment on the mule to draw its attention away from the pain that would be inflicted on its hooves. The mule's owner often was summoned to help with this procedure.

Most of the farmers tried to have this kind of work done before the spring plowing and planting got underway, but the best laid plans were not always good enough. A lot of the time in hot weather an old farmer or his young son would be seen pulling on a rope with an one real ole mule hobbling along on the end of it up the road to get a horseshoe replaced or repaired, and while he was there he'd bring along a plow or tool that needed repairing. I'm sure the poor ole blacksmith was not overly enthused at that sight.

When the hoof (or hooves) had been repaired, if the old nag was gentle enough we'd ride on her back home, not a real comfortable ride but a different experience.

A lot of wagon wheels were always waiting to be repaired along with several smaller items like irons with broken handles or singletrees that connected the plows with the plowstocks.1f our Dad or Mom found a real lightweight object that needed repairing, they'd let us smaller kids run the errand. While we were there and waiting we'd saunter around and pick up a few of the bigger chunks of coal to take home and pour mercurochrome and salt and bluing over it to grow some beautiful colorful formations.

As fall approached, many people had to have a few "firedogs" (andirons) repaired or made and the tongs with which they chunked the fires would break or get warped and need repairing. A few of the more gifted blacksmiths would create handsome door hinges and trivets or cutting blades and improvised digging hoes. He could even style some hanging racks to be erected in the open fireplaces to hang iron kettles or pots from.

These "old world" items were still used by some families, and in most instances saved wood as a few foods could be cooked over the fire. In the winter when these fires were going full blast we would also stick potatoes in the big bank of ashes in the fireplace to be baked. These were turned regularly with some of the tongs that our local blacksmith had concocted.

It's hard to visualize a man in his right mind desiring to become a blacksmith, with all that intense heat and grimy coal smoke to endure, especially when he knew of the very skimpy compensation they received.

.

Sharpening Up The Tools By Hand

In January or February on a sunny day when it wasn't too cold and our Dad would allow it, was a good time to sharpen up all the dulled blades we had propped up in the corner of the wagon shed.

He'd don his old fabric cap with the fold over the bill, put on his overall jacket, find his rusty metal file and start assembling all the axes, hoes, mowing blades and cross-cut saws he could find and pile them down by the back porch steps. This was the same place he had used for that purpose for years.

Often he'd call me to sit on the handles to steady them while he sharpened each one to his specifications. I had to find a cap and sweater, as the weather was kinda chilly when you weren't exercising.

Dad could never quite get started without a few choice descriptive slang remarks. I loved them; they were almost always some combinations I'd never heard before, and I could tell he wasn't really mad, just letting off a little steam, which was normal for him.

After a little fanfare he'd get settled down on his knees all hunkered over the selected blade and start scraping away. He'd use both hands for some places, but only one for the corners or most tedious places. However, no effort was exerted without his mouth being positioned just right. He'd hold his lips crooked to one side of his mouth and really grind down with that old metal file.

At intervals he had me move over so he could take up the axe or hoe to inspect them carefully so he could see what else needed to be done. As soon as it was laid back down I'd resume my seat and we were right back in business.

Sometimes we'd be interrupted by the crows flying over or a hawk's screech. Both of these predators took top priority, as my Dad tried real hard to eliminate them from our farm. He hopped up as fast as he could and hurried to find and load his double-barreled shotgun only to find they'd flown away in the meantime. After this disappointment he just parked the old gun real close to our filing operation in case they showed up again.

After we'd sharpened two or three of the smaller tools he'd be exhausted, so we'd stop and get a drink of water, after which he had to chew a wad of tobacco, which seemed to be a tranquilizer for a few minutes, then it was back to the proverbial "grindstone."

There was no conversation involved. He had his mouth all set for the job and I didn't have anything to say so I just sat there and watched him change facial expressions and learned how to sharpen tools. A few times, if the handles had been around a long time and had been in active duty they would crack under all that strain, so this would precipitate some more of those unusual slang words. Of course, he had to go find a new handle, which never fit as it was. He had to whittle around and pound and bump around on them till he figured it would be "dig-worthy" before he put it down. Then we'd finish sharpening that one and move on to bigger and worser things.

He always left the big ole scary looking crosscut saw till last. We both dreaded that one. If I didn't sit on it just right those long jagged teeth would bite my legs, and it was very hard to sit still with one of them jabbing me. If I moved at the wrong time, I was the object of some of them unusual sharp words, and no matter how used I was to hearing them I always felt hurt when they were directed at me. That long saw with a handle on each end was hard to manipulate. I had to help turn it over and let him check it out to see where it needed more work. There were several rest periods and it took a lot of tobacco to finish that job.

When the sun was no longer warm and Dad was worn out, we'd hang it all up for that day. After we had separated the sharpened tools from the ones we hadn't worked on, we put them all back where they belonged till another time when there wasn't anything else more important to do. Most of the smaller items were sharpened on a grindstone, which was most likely faster and certainly more to my approval.

When Bees Swarmed

Honey was a really important food in our neck of the woods. It didn't cost anything, and once you captured the bees and made them a permanent, comfortable home, you only needed to develop a little courage so that at a specified time you could gather the honey which they had produced.

Most of the farmers around us had their own bee hives set up around the edges of their pastures or yards, and several of them had a lot of hives, hoping to sell some of the honey.

In the spring when the rainiest season was over and the weather began to get warm, some of the bees would swarm (move, en masse, out of their old hives led by the queen bee) in search of a new more desirable abode. A whole family of bees looked like a tight wad of bugs in flight, except they made a distinctive noise, resembling bees in a jug or a low-pitched buzz saw. They moved rapidly along, alarming all who saw them, often settling in a big bundle around a tree limb. A farmer having caught a glimpse of them would try real hard to follow them, hoping to add them to his own collection.

As soon as the bees seemed settled, the farmer would yell for someone to bring him a baited bee hive and all the other things it took to lure them to his hive. The new hive was placed on an old sheet underneath the bundle of bees, at which time the limb was jarred hard enough to dismantle the whole colony. The frightened and upset bees, smelling the syrup-lined hive below, usually made their "bee line" to get into the new home.

It took a lot of courage for those men to get that close to a zillion angry bees, which were zinging all around them, often lighting on their clothes and hats, as they inspected everything close by while deciding which way to go.

With a lot of patience and precision and skillful persuading, the bees were finally coaxed into the hive and got calmed down enough to start taking orders from the queen bee. After several days, the farmer, with several helpers, very carefully moved this new family near the other bee hives, where a near normal existence prevailed.

No one was ever sure where the bees came from nor why. They could have come from the forest or from a distant neighbor's house. Maybe queen bee #1 didn't like her nosy neighbor, queen bee #2, or perhaps one of them thought their workers was spending too much time at their competitor's hives; or maybe they just got their hive good and dirty and decided to move, like some of the sharecroppers did. At any rate, the farmer was proud of his new possessions, as the bees hurried around hunting nectar for a fresh crop of honey.

When the trees and flowers had stopped blooming, a farmer would help the bees produce honey by putting out old sugared syrup, discolored old honey, or even sugar, for them to use in their honeycombs. Most of the kids had been stung by a bee at some time and place, so the bee hives were widely respected by them and the women folk, who had a natural tendency to fight at them if they got too close, which, of course, made the bees angry and a lot more likely to sting someone.

When someone got stung, the most often used remedy was a little wad of chewed tobacco placed directly on the spot. Most stings were not serious, resulting only in a red swollen lump, which later got feverish and then started itching. However, a few highly sensitive people suffered terrible reactions even to death, when there were multiple stings around the head, so this made everyone uneasy when the bees started flying too close.

Some men were natural born bee handlers who knew exactly how to handle them even to robbing their hives. These men, with their proper attire, were in great demand when honey gathering time came. Their pay was usually swapped labor or a portion of the honey they collected. In most cases a smoke torch was used in collecting the honey combs from the hives, as well as from the trees in the forests. The smoke kept the bees at bay, making them leave their hives, hence, the hive-robber's job was a lot easier and safer this way.

The gooey, nasty looking super-sweet stuff was removed from the hive and hastily dumped into a large pail. The pail was carried inside the house and emptied into a larger container to be sorted by one of the women. The prettiest and clearest honey with its comb was put in one pail or jar while the darkest, with possible unhatched eggs, was placed in another pan. The very worst, darkest honey was carried back out to the other hives to be recycled by the bees themselves.

All of the liquid that had leaked out of the combs was strained and stored in glass containers to be used for cooking or sweetening beverages or just as a spread for hot bread and butter. It was all raw honey and not always as clear and pretty as that we buy today at the grocery store, but it served the same purpose, plus it had special healing powers for stubborn sores that were hard to heal. It was used for this purpose as a last resort.

Cotton Pickin' Time

On the hottest days of summer just after "August meetin", there were a few not -so-busy days preceding the really hard jobs that an early harvest always ushered in. These were some of the few days that we had to half-way relax and play in the "branch," cut watermelons, or just sit and swing or rock to try to keep cool. This was also the time when we had to help our Mother gather and can fruits and vegetables before cotton opened enough to pick and before school started.

The cotton crop was by far the most important thing on our agenda. Our Dad had purchased seeds, fertilizer, and many other household items which were to be paid for when we "sold our cotton."

The infamous cotton was not just planted and picked, there was a long period of time in between when we had to thin, weed, and fertilize it all by hand. There were also those little pests called boll-weevils that could really upset the apple cart. Our Dad kept a close vigil on them and the weeds. When he noticed either of them getting a hold he'd hurry home and round up the whole work force and start attacking with whatever it took. For the weeds, it took a lot of hoeing, and for the boll-weevils we carried little jars around to pick up the defective squares that had fallen from the plants because the bugs had infested them. We'd burn them at the edge of the fields, trying to curb the weevils, but often we'd have to put out poison to do away with them.

If we had a rainy summer the weevils and grass were both a lot worse, so it was hard for us to be thankful for all the rainy weather. Cotton was at its best when the bolls were large and fluffy. The weather played a big part, but we were also a big contributor to its well-being by keeping it weeded, de-bugged and fertilized.

At the beginning of the season it was exciting to see the first bolls start to crack open with a little bit of white showing! By this time we had already started getting our cotton sacks ready. For this our Mom would collect the

186

fertilizer bags which we had kept for this purpose, wash them real good and dry them and then measure up each person for his or her right size. The material was strong and tightly woven, so it lasted well and was fairly easy to sew. The bags had a wide strap that went in front of one shoulder and behind the other, with the outer side of the bag opening larger at about your hips height. The bottoms of the bag were just above the ground so as not to wear a hole in it as you dragged it along.

The sun being very hot and bright precipitated our digging out those straw hats one more time. We were also forced to find some old worn out shoes to keep the ground heat from burning our feet.

We started off with exuberance and gusto in a big competitive spirit; for some reason or other each of us wanted to pick the most cotton. That young, "straw-hatted" brigade must have been quite a sight marching off on that "cotton pickin' safari," all fitted out with those big bags to haul in their prey.

Everything went according to plan except when an unsuspecting member happened upon some tall cotton infested with "stinging worms." These little monsters were camouflaged to match the cotton stalks and leaves, and were well fortified with the most efficient stinging bristles nature could provide. The worms were long and roundish and completely covered with those itchy, stingy bristles, which everyone tried desperately to avoid.

As soon as one was spied, or felt, the whole kit and kaboodle came to seek them out and destroy them no matter how much chase it involved. Often a sizable area would be infected with them and sometimes more than one person would be stung. This always slowed the cotton picking considerably 'cause we spent more time checking for worms than we did picking cotton.

The handiest treatment for these stings was tobacco juice. Our Dad always had a ready supply on hand. When we got home at night and bathed we'd put camphor on the area, and usually by morning the worst part was over.

When things were back to normal we'd hurry to fill our bags with cotton so we could walk to the nearest basket to empty them. This let us straighten our backs and stretch. These baskets were rather large like three feet tall and about two or three feet across. When they were about full one of the smaller kids would climb in and pack the cotton real hard so we could put in some more. Everyone would volunteer for that job. Soon we'd have two large baskets full and our grown brothers would lift them up and balance them on one shoulder and carry them home to our cotton house. During the main season this house would be about half full of pretty white fluffy cotton and every chance we got we would roll and tumble in it. It was awfully hot in there but the soft cotton made a good cushion for those somersaults.

When we had our cotton all picked and weren't too busy otherwise, our neighbors would ask us to help them gather theirs. We were usually delighted, as this was one of the few sources to earn money out in the boonies. At their cotton fields our bags were weighed when they got full and a running total was kept of each one's harvest. We really tried hard to outdo each other here so someone would brag on us *and* we'd get that much more money! The money we earned was extremely meager, but it went a long way, not to mention that it was hard for the farmer to scrounge up any cash to pay us with.

At home we could hardly wait to help load the picked cotton onto the wagon with its tall sides put up. From previous experience our Dad and brothers knew when we had loaded enough for a whole bale on the wagon. At that time we'd crawl up on top and ride to the cotton gin to watch it get processed. It was very exciting to see how the cotton got de-seeded, packed tight and baled with metal straps and a burlap cover all ready to sell and apply to our ongoing charges at the company store.

Picnics In The Wilds

As sure as the beautiful spring weather appeared, with the warm sun casting those short shadows, everyone was restless and ready to do something different on the outside.

By this time of year the gardens were planted, the flowers had been put out of the house and some of the crops had been planted. It was definitely barefoot time, and the school year was coming to a close.

The teacher always tried to do something special just before the end of school, and a picnic was almost always selected as the favorite. There was never any squabbling over the place; the official picnic grounds had been established years ago. It was too far to walk we'd go by car or mule and wagon express. We loved riding on the wagon with our feet hanging off the back end.

There were no picnic tables here, so each family brought a cloth and spread it on the grass and weighted it down with our food and eating paraphernalia. These picnic grounds were in a cow pasture with a beautiful 'small stream that ran close by. Weeds didn't grow very tall in that area since the grass was not fertilized and the "cow mowers" kept it cropped off pretty short, enabling us to see where we were walking as well as everything else close by.

There were trees leaning across the creek that we could climb around on and that stream of water was so tempting we all wound up in there. Mostly we'd play hide-n-seek or "Jack Stones" or batting a ball. We never ran out of something to do to entertain ourselves while our parents and the teachers caught up with their story telling and tattling.

The food was never really a surprise. We had the same things year after year. There must have been at least six dishes of deviled eggs, four or five potato salads, at least three platters of salmon patties, some homegrown salty ham and about three platters of fried chicken. From that meat source, we'd move on to the few vegetables and salads. The thing we liked the very best were the desserts. There were sweet potato pies, tea cakes, muffins, cobbler pies, caramel cake, chocolate cake, and banana pudding. All of those were our favorites, and we always overate. As long as there was food left we'd keep sneaking back to get another taste. As one girl put it, some of it "tasted better than it looked."

Table manners were strictly left at home for these functions. We reached around and in front of each other to get our favorite foods before they were all gone, and we weren't too complimentary; if something didn't taste good to us, we said so or flung it out across the pasture.

The Sunday schools, not to be outdone, would also have an annual picnic at the same place with basically the same foods and same crowd, but we enjoyed them too and looked forward to them each year. One day at our house when our parents were gone for the day we got an urge to go on our own picnic. Some of the older ones had heard of a nice place on a creek different from the one where all the others were held. The idea was mighty appealing, but it was too far to walk, so we hit on the idea of going in the wagon. The only "man" around to hitch up the mules to the wagon was our youngest brother, who was only 8-10 years old, but he knew how it went so the rest of us got busy, fetched some soda crackers and peanut butter and a few other morsels that were edible to be topped off with lemonade.

After all the preparations we piled the food and ourselves into the wagon, grabbed the reins of the team of mules and coaxed and "giddy-upped" them till they decided to move out, heading for brand new territory. We rode down the road a mile or two and struck out into a wooded area in search of "that creek" we'd been told about.

It was a little difficult driving that wagon through the woods around and over the bushes, but we were doing fine till the wagon got hung up on an old tree stump. The mules stopped short and started nickering, which upset us all. After a few minutes when we'd quieted them down, we crawled off the wagon and discovered what the problem was. After unhitching the mules we shoved and pushed and pulled and turned the wagon till we got it unlodged.

By this time, we were fussing, perspiring, aggravated, and thirsty, so we dragged out everything we had brought along to eat and went through all of it in very short order. Then we hitched up the mules one more time and made a beeline for the road that led to home. We never did find "that creek" but we did find the mosquitoes and poison oak, plus the whole escapade sufficed for a long time to discourage those impromptu picnics in unknown places.

Fish Fries In The Rough

On a really hot summer day it was not unusual for my folks to get in touch with some of our kinfolk to meet for a fish fry at the river that was near their house. No one ever doubted that the fish would not be there nor caught. This "feed bag" was strictly planned and programmed on faith.

The method for catching fish for this occasion was seining. It was a hard and often dangerous procedure: walking up the river with its uneven bottom and large unseeable rocks and maybe even trees that had fallen, carrying those heavy nets. That was the only sure-fire way of producing enough fish for the hungry crowd.

If it happened the weather was nice and hot the kids would also wade in the shallow edges of the river and play splashing each other. When you left home for the fish fry you packed eating apparatus, cooking utensils, salt, meal, lard, iced tea and maybe a little other food, but mostly we were dependent on the fish for food.

In preparation the men rounded up a pair of old worn out overalls and shoes to wear in the river. If this location had been near a railroad track, anyone catching a glimpse of this motley crew in their ragged get-up would have mistaken them for hobos.

The nets used were large and strong and had to be carried by several able bodied men, while a few others went upstream and drove the fish down toward the net. At intervals the nets were closed up and dragged ashore to see what the catch of the day was.

Everyone gathered around with high hopes. Much to our bewilderment there would be a lot of water varmints flipping and thrashing around. The cache consisted mostly of catfish (blue and mudcat) some of them weighing as much as 7-10 lbs. with monstrous heads. In fact, the heads were bigger than their bodies. There were also perch and some other scale fish, but the most interesting thing in the net was a water snake or two and

192

at least one eel. Every now and then they'd capture a turtle.

These last three were the ones that captivated us kids. The snakes would be killed and flung out in the woods but all the other creatures would be cleaned and prepared for cooking (except for the turtle). If the fish haul did not produce enough fish for supper, the same process of seining would be carried out again.

While the men were in the river trying to drive the fish into the net, the women and kids would be bringing up limbs and sticks to make a fire. Most of the time we'd bring some additional wood from home to be sure to have a hot enough fire.

This place had been used for fish fries so much that someone had stacked rocks up with room for a fire in between stacks, and placed an iron rack on top so there'd be a good place to set the big black fry pans. Some of the women and small boys cleaned the fish, washed the meat real good and salted it down so as to be ready to cook when the coals had burned down to the right look. The fry pans were filled with grease and as they heated the fish were rolled in meal and dunked into the hot grease. The smell was wonderful and was carried a long way into the wooded area making everyone hungry.

The weather was already hot and the humidity was terrible so the heat from standing over the hot fires was hard to endure, but everyone had his job and manned his station and the supper was well underway.

The men quit seining when it was decided they had enough fish to feed the crowd so they would grapple under the river banks for turtles. Most of the time they'd bring out two or three extra turtles, which they would throw in a tub with the other one and add a little water to keep them alive till we got them home. The smallest kids would play poking them with sticks to see how long the turtle would hold on. Those funny looking sharp snouts would really clamp down on those sticks and the mamas had to keep close watch to make sure the kids didn't get bitten. Word was that if they bit you they wouldn't let go till it thundered, and we sure didn't want one hanging on to us that long?!

We kids would all gather around the cooking place when the mothers started to fry the eel and the fish eggs. The eggs sounded like fire-crackers when they hit that hot grease and we'd all jump back so the hot grease would not hit us. Then when the eel was dumped in the pan it would wiggle. We considered that to be funny.

As soon as the fish were all fried up and the hushpuppies had been cooked, we'd prepare the plates and drinks in order to be ready to "dig in" as soon as possible. Every time we passed by the fish we'd pinch off a bite and keep traveling. The cornbread was even better. Sometimes we weren't very hungry when the real call to eat came.

When everything was ready and everyone had found a place to sit, we gorged ourselves and reflected on the seining experience and tried to figure out who really deserved the credit for the biggest fish.

It didn't dawn on us that we were rapidly collecting a big supply of chiggers as well as high cholesterol and a blood pressure problem. We were just living for the moment.

August Meeting 'A Country

Our country church had only one revival a year, in August and they came to be known as the "August Meetings." Every little church in our area held theirs at about the same time, or within a week of each other. This particular time was selected because most of the crops had been laid by, the garden contributions had been preserved, the blackberries had been picked and the fall harvest items were not quite ready to be gathered.

A lot of preparations had to be made for these "protracted" meetings as each service day and night had to be attended and the preachers (at least two of them) had to be housed and fed by the church membership. A lot of housecleaning had to be done, clothes mended or even some new ones made, chickens fattened, hair permed or washed and styled along with the general lingo improved. Nothing was more embarrassing than coming out with a cuss word in front of the preachers or other important company which visited around generously during this week.

Some of us kids or our Mom would nearly always need some new shoes just for this occasion and for the next communities meeting. We liked to attend them all if it were at all possible. By the time they were all over we were so revived we could hardly go another day and looked awfully bedraggled from all the rushing around and sweating and pretending.

When the revival finally formally commenced the whole community united in a friendly. concerted effort to show their readiness to cooperate to the fullest in whatever programs those highly respected reverends recommended. Even though these men-of-the-cloth were unlearned and often unrighteous persons we still looked up to them and were ready for them to lead us all to higher ground.

We had worked hard all year, had very little to look forward to in the way of material things and were anxiously anticipating a real spiritual rebirth, or at the least being revived along with a reprieve from our humdrum hard work routines.

Wherever the preachers went for dinner or supper, some of the neighbors were invited to come along and help entertain them. We were very awkward and ill-at-ease in the presence of the clergy so any support we could acquire from some of our neighbors was deeply appreciated and needed. It was always a relief when the preachers dismissed themselves and went off to a room or for a walk by themselves. It gave us a chance to regroup and whisper around about our opinions of them as we ran to the toilets or sneaked a bite to eat before they returned, often for supper at the same house.

The women were worn to a frazzle as they hurried around in the extremely hot kitchens cooking up a lot of food for the crowds, morning and evenings. Those pore ole chicken coops got emptied up during these revivals. That was the only fresh meat that could be prepared without going fishing and no one had time for that, they were expected to attend those meetings. As the week wore on and the screaming pastors began to get hoarse and the witnessing brethren and sistren were worn out from going through their repetitious experiences and the singers had completely devastated "Almost Persuaded," "Just As I Am" and "Jesus Paid It All", all of the younger kids who had not previously joined the church began to get fidgety about the need to go up for prayer or pretend they'd been saved before that series of meetings was over.

The parents would glance around at their offspring hoping they'd take that final step, while the offspring would squirm around in their seats and whisper or giggle with their friends lest they really felt convicted and walked up to the altar to be prayed over.

Eventually one of the kids would go boldly to the preacher and ask to "join the church" while his friends followed in rapid succession, whether led by the spirit or not, they weren't gonna be glared at any more by their peers nor were they gonna be left out when the others got baptized. Some of the parents must have been suspicious about their child's rebirth for they got right up out of their seats and came to the front and knelt with their child and started patting on them, raising their arms and praying out loud as though the savior was hard of hearing. These actions often precipitated a mad rush to the altar by half the congregation to help pray those penitent children to heaven.

At times it looked like they were trying to beat the devil out of them. It sure was a relief when one of those kids hopped up and said he'd been saved, of course all of the others responded with the same conclusion as fast as they could get up. The ecstatic preachers wasted no time calling it a miracle and shouting "Praise the Lord" At that instant the organ busted a loose with "I Surrender All" or "What A Friend We Have in Jesus" or "Power in the Blood," while all the main singers sang along as they remembered the words. At this time almost the whole congregation went up to hug and shake hands with each of the new converts offering them all kinds of advice on how to live and be a shining example to all the other kids.

Eventually the service was closed out for the night and the crowd headed for home, eager to spread the word about little James or Flora being saved to those who had the misfortune of not being able to attend that service. Each new "convert" brought added interest for the next service till the crowds were too big for the church, which already had poor air circulation.

Those funeral parlor fans were well worth their cost (usually free) during those steamy, sweaty meetings (before the advent of deodorants), as everyone fanned himself and the person seated by him furiously while they wiped the sweat and pulled at their dampened garments that had got stuck here and there, sometimes in terribly embarrassing places.

The onlookers came from far and near and milled in and out of the church peering through the open windows and doors like this was gonna be their last chance to surrender all. All of this outrageous behavior certainly took away from the sacredness of the service as the last

days approached. But not to worry, there was gonna be a
whole new revival starting up down the road about six
miles and the whole procedure was sure to be repeated
only bigger and better till August was over. The only
thing barring our being there was time out to fix up a
turnip patch or a bad case of the "runs."

Bugs And Games With Them

May was a nice month in every respect, the weather was warm, the early flowers were blooming, the grass was greening up in the pastures and a lot of gardening had been done. School was not quite out but the spring fever had set in and everyone felt energetic and ready to get underway with all the outside activities.

When we were outside for any length of time, we'd see butterflies checking out the bright blossoms that were now on the scene. We'd watch and admire them with great interest for awhile; we'd count them, describe them, compare them and point them out to each other till our curiosity got the best of us, then we'd start sneaking up on them to try to catch them just for the satisfaction of being able to show them to our mom or sisters and brothers.

Later we started creeping up on all of them we could reach, grabbing them by the wings between our thumb and index fingers. The iridescent coloring on their wings would rub off on our hands and we were elated by that new discovery. We'd also catch a few and keep them in jars or pin them to boards. Then we'd yank one wing off to see if they could fly with only one wing, or we'd pinch off their antennas to see if they could manipulate that way, but as soon as our mother saw us torturing and killing them she'd shame us and "dare" us to catch another one.

With that game coming to a screeching halt we had to find something else to play. We weren't too good at catching bumble bees, plus they kinda fought back and we wound up running from them. With the entrance of June, we were eagerly awaiting the arrival of the June bugs. The first to find one made the news known to everyone everywhere as we scoured all of the weeds and bushes in search of a big active one for our very own. Our reason for finding them was so we could tie a long string to one of their hind legs and let him try to flyaway as we held on to the other end of the string. We played this game for a long time or till the June bug ran out of steam. Those tough shelled beautifully colored bugs made havoc with the flowers and vegetable plants so our parents did not mind our playing with them or destroying them for that matter. With the passing of June that game was over so we had to find some other way to amuse ourselves.

The dirt dobbers were considered a nuisance by our peers so they tried to interest us in knocking them down with a broom and watching them drop their little ball of mud or the little live insect they had captured for their mud pantries. Very often they'd construct a long narrow mud house on the ceilings or some other hard to reach place. We loved the challenge of jabbing the nests down. We worked and worked at the wrecking job till we had completely destroyed their houses and supply of still-living insects.

Sometimes we would hardly get one house torn down before they'd start another. As they plastered the mud on the surface they'd make a real distinct buzz. We all knew that sound and would rally with our long sticks to tear up any new building they'd put up.

In spite of our vigil they wound up building mud tunnels over and on several walls or window sills or ceilings, which often went undetected for weeks.

As summer wore on the season for lightning bugs approached and endowed us with a brand new idea for something to do. They seemed to produce rapidly for I'm sure we caught and "canned up" all of the first 500 that arrived. We had our own personal glass canning jars with a fitted and ventilated (holes poked in) lid. Inside of them we first put some greenery for them to forage on as well as providing some natural surroundings for them to move around on. As long as we could see or guess at where they were when they'd turn their lights off we'd grabble for them. It was a lot of fun seeing who could catch the most. When the lids were opened to put in the new one we had just caught, about two would crawl out so it took a long time to accumulate many of them.

Our mother fretted each night when we were running around barefoot afraid of our being bit by a snake. When we'd finally come inside after it was too dark to see which way to go, she'd fret because the lightning bugs were escaping from the jars and flying all over the house, ready to light up and disturb her sleep. Unfortunately the lightning bug season was short lived too.

The only other bug entertainment I recall was watching ants wander around with big loads in their mouths, hunting the shortest cut back to their underground tunnels. They acted like they were blind as they retraced their trails over and over till they made a little forward progress. You wanted to help them but they were too stupid to learn. Mostly we didn't have enough patience to pursue that hobby.

But we were captivated by the little doodle bug holes that we found in many sandy areas. We'd find a small stick and gently stir the dirt around the little hole in the ground as we chanted "doodle bug, doodle bug, come out of the ground, your house is on fire." Most of the time we'd stir the little funny looking bug out of his hole, but he usually just tunneled right back down using his backend to tunnel.

Most of the "bug" games were seasonal and just as well cause our interest spans were kinda short lived anyway.

Hog Killing Episodes

Hog killing was as vital a part of our yearly survival cycle as gardening since these big ogres supplied the most of our meat for at least six months of the year. Just as the coastal people depended on fish and the mid-westerners depended on beef, we were the "pork people." With our household running over with grown boys (or men), we had our own slaughtering crew for this strenuous task. Many families with only one man in the household had to coordinate a plan with his neighbors to help each other.

After having fed and fattened the hogs for almost a year, we were all ready for the November cold to come along so we could let the hogs start feeding us for a change. This of course the ole hogs knew nothing about, and none of us told them - not even at the last minute.

When the temperature was cold enough (freezing to be exact), Dad would sharpen up all the big butcher knives, axes, get a big supply of salt, set up the sausage grinder, erect the outside scaffolding, build a hot fire under the black pot full of water and march the crew out to the hog pen where they'd kill the ole unsuspecting hog. Then they dragged him to the boiling pot and scaffolding and poured the hot water all over the carcass so they could scrape all the hair from the whole body.

At this time it was ready to be hoisted up on the scaffolding and relieved of all its innards. We kids would watch for a while and then run back inside with our hands over our mouths.

Pretty soon our Dad would start yelling for someone to come get the liver or some of the chitterlings (intestines), which we took to the branch and started cleaning and washing. There was always a lot of argument about who was gonna have to do that nasty job, but as soon as someone was settled on, they got busy and got all the necessary utensils together and got underway. We sure needed a clothespin for our noses for that job. As soon as they looked pretty clean we left them to soak in a tub full of water and added a handful of baking soda to help lessen the odor. Dad sure wanted us kids to eat those chitterlings, but no amount of pay, no persuasion could accomplish that. One of our little brothers (only two) got hold of some of them, all battered and fried up, and swung them backward and forward in his little forefingers and blurted out "ling, ling guts." This brought a chorus of laughter which even came from our Dad and Mother. I think he slackened his selling job on the chitterlings after that.

By the time we got back to the house, the men had the big frame lowered and were whacking away on first one part and then another. There were about five or six different containers for all the various parts. The head was plopped in one, along with the tail and feet; the side meat and ribs and tenderloin were put in another; the shoulders and hams in another, with all the fat and skins in a separate one to be used for making lard, and lastly, all of the little bits and pieces and leftovers were all grouped together in a separate place for sausage.

The whole process was the mess of messes. The fresh meat and blood scents always nauseated about half of us, but we had to keep working. The meat had to be processed and preserved as quickly as possible, so the cold weather could cure it before it spoiled. There had been occasions when the weather turned warm too fast and some of the meat spoiled. We couldn't afford that, as much as we needed these supplemental delicacies for our Christmas feasting.

Before all of the refuse had been thrown away, one of our brothers would clean off the bladder and give it to us for a balloon. To achieve this treat we found a small reed, inserted it into the end and blew it up.

Sometimes we could play with it for hours before it deflated or tore up. Our Mom was awfully interested in cleaning and cooking the head, feet and tail so she could make pressed meat. She also doted on that plagued liver mush. The kids all hated the smell of liver cooking and were extremely glad when she got that over. The pressed meat looked good, but knowing what was in it made it another no-no.

The hams and at least one shoulder along with all the side meat wound up in a big wooden box with salt, where it stayed for several days or weeks. One of the tastiest items was the wonderful tenderloin with gravy and hot biscuits which we always ate for supper the day we killed our hogs. Another favorite was the spareribs which our Mom could cook to perfection.

The sausage meat, which we all liked, took forever to grind and regrind and season and then stuff into little bags or chitterlings to cure. For the sausage our Mom sewed up long skinny cloth bags which we used for stuffing the small wads of ground meat in, one little wad at a time and squeezed to the bottom. T'was a long, greasy job, but with several folks working at it we did get it all stuffed and hung up to start curing in the smokehouse. The chitterlings were even harder to stuff resulting in a smaller amount of them.

Last on the long list of disposing of the body parts was placing the skins in the oven and fat scraps in the big black pot to simmer down for lard. The pork skins when degreased and crisp were delicious, and we waited anxiously for them to get done while the fatty scraps simmered in the big black pot till it all seemed to turn into liquid. At this point the lard was poured up in large tin containers with tight fitting lids till it solidified into a greasy white shortening ready for cooking and frying all our foodstuffs. A big fat hog produced a lot of lard which was necessary for shortening to be used all year, if it lasted that long.

The hams which were strictly used for company fare were hung up in the smokehouse after sufficient curing and seasoning in the wooden salt boxes, The side meat was kept salted down till it was needed for seasoning veggies or for bacon. Some of us ate so much pork we looked like "little porkers."

Some of the best fresh meat was sorted out and hand delivered to our neighbors who reciprocated as soon as they killed their hogs. It was always interesting to see if they sent us the same choice meat that we had sent them.

Luckily most of this meat was gone before the weather got hot the next year when the chickens were big enough for us to eat. During all that time we kept our fingers crossed, hoping our Mother would not come up with some way to use the pigs "squeal" and "hoofs."

Corn Shuckings

Shucking corn and corn shuckings were two completely different things. Shucking com was an everyday task that was engaged in for human and animal consumption, while corn shuckings were special occasions that were held when an abundance of corn needed shucking.

When the roasting ears (young fresh corn) were in season, we'd often run out to the com patch and pick about a dozen ears to bring home where we shucked them to be cooked for dinner or supper. It was as if we had planted at least one juicy worm with every seed of corn, cause we never opened up a shuck where there wasn't a worm waiting in there just to scare the stuffin' out of us. We'd screech and often throw the ear down as soon as we'd spot him, at best we'd shake the corn till the worm fell out and we could stomp him.

As soon as our brothers heard all the noise, they'd come running and pretend to find a worm to chase us with. Those chases would go on and on before our Mom would hear all the commotion and come to our rescue, and, of course, make us all get back to work. We (girls) were actually more afraid of those little wiggly worms than we were of snakes. When the corn was grown and had been picked from the dried up stalks, it was shucked on a daily basis for pigs, chickens, and mules to eat.

For the chickens and pigs we had to also shell the corn. This was kinda rough on the palms of our hands, as the kernels were rubbed off the ears with our bare hands. Just a few ears of corn was no problem, but a sizable pan full of ears could almost make a blister on our hands. The only good part was there were no worms.

The mules had to remove their own corn from the cob. 'Twas a funny scene to watch them chewing with so much motion, as they waddled the kernels from one side of their mouth to the other. Our Dad loved to show us how a "mule ate com" by pinching up a big wad of skin on one of our outstretched kneecaps and wiggling the loose skin between his thumb and forefinger. The little kids thought it was funny, but after you were 12 years or older, the funny had worn off.

When our Mom decided to make hominy, we would sit down and shell a whole bunch of corn, de-weeviling it as we went. Weevils were little bugs that loved to bore into the kernels. Corn to be used for corn meal was our biggest job. Dad would often help us with that, as our corn sheller usually didn't work worth a doodle. He usually knew some funny tale he'd either heard or made up, and that kept us entertained.

The cleaning up took us about as long as the actual corn shelling, as we had to carry those shucks to the cow pasture and throw them over for the cows to eat. When we carried too big a load and some of them fell, we'd most likely say, "Aw-shucks!" As soon as we had carried off all the shucks, we'd have to pile the cobs in a big tub to be used for kindling.

When we took small amounts to be ground for corn meal, our Dad would let us ride on the wagon to the mill. One of our brothers worked at the corn mill for a short while, so we felt free to go in the mill and watch. There was an awful lot of dust flying all over the place, so we'd have to knock it off our clothes and hair when we went out. We also got to go in the store for some marble candy before we started home. That was our pay for all the work, and we held on to those marbles forever.

The bona fide "corn shuckings" were a whole different ball game. They involved several grownup men who were intent on getting a lot of corn shucked in a short time.

The custom in some communities was to hide a jug of "white lightning" whiskey in the bottom of a tall pile of corn that was still in the husks, and when the job was over, all of the participants would celebrate with that potent brew. As the afternoon wore on, each person would peel open and shuck dozens of ears of corn, which they graded as they went. The biggest and best ears were saved for planting the next year, so it was put aside from the other corn, which was thrown over in a big rat -proof bin. Many times the shucking was interrupted and

207

turned into a full-fledged rat killing. The rats always nested in or near the corn crib, so everyone was on guard for a rat to hop out.

There was some real fast action when one of them ran out and tried to make a fast getaway. These men were very adept at rat killing, and one of the little boogers very seldom got away. They got clobbered with a foot, a stick or an ear of corn, or anything else that would serve as a weapon. There should have been a prize given to the one who bagged the most rats. If left alone, these rodents could do a lot of damage to the corn crop as well as the other seeds and feed. A few dogs were trained to catch them, but they were too big for the cats to tangle with, even though they were kept around for that purpose.

If one man was faster and shucked more corn than the others, it didn't take him long to start teasing the others with, "I done shucked two to yawl's one." Of course that precipitated a lot of conversations about each person's misgivings; from there they'd tell tall tales about fishing episodes or hunting happenings, and then they'd get on with some jokes that some of them thought were funny.

At intervals each person would chew a fresh bite of tobacco or smoke a fast home-rolled cigarette and go out behind the barn to relieve himself before returning to the unfinished pile of corn. When the pile was really slim, someone would spot the whiskey jug and a big whoopee erupted from everyone as they all grabbed for the handle.

This, of course, brought an abrupt end to the corn shucking, as the jug got passed around to everyone who could stomach that strong whiskey. As soon as each man had had several slugs of "licker", they managed to clean up the shucks before they finished off the booze and headed for home.

It was rumored that one robust but gentle man was quite inebriated when he staggered home and immediately fell across the bed. He had a tiny wife who didn't like booze in the first place, so she took advantage of this opportunity to roll him up in the bedspread and proceed

208

to wallop him a few whacks with his razor strap. Bet that made him take second thoughts about going to another corn shucking and indulging in that corn whiskey.

Plotting The Preserves

Our Mom simply had not finished her spring and summer rituals if she had not canned a couple of gallons of fig and pear preserves (these were our favorites).

The fig bush at our house was not very prolific. Matter of fact, it scarcely grew in size either; it was about the same size for about 10years. But one of our closest neighbors had a huge one that always had bushels of figs on it every year, and that family didn't like them in the first place. Theirs were all for giving away to anyone who'd come and gather them. Seeing as how fig preserves were such a treat to us, we weren't about to let the birds and bees have all those figs. So, whenever the season was right we'd make ourselves plentiful around their house, hoping to be invited to help ourselves to the figs.

At such a time, we'd approach the big bush with a small pail so as to not look piggish, but when the neighbor saw us coming they would bring a dishpan out to us and often help us pick them. The bees and birds had also been observing the ripening process and many of the ripest and largest figs had already been pecked into or had three or four bees sitting on them nibbling away on the tender, sweet meat.

The ones that were too near eaten up were left but we saved a lot of the ones with small bites on them. The brittle, large branches were hard to pull over so we could gather the ones furtherest up. Guess that's why the older gent had stuck around to help us out in that respect. When he wasn't around, we'd taste of the ripest ones and invariably spit it out. The taste was simply not to our liking. Our Mom would not have wanted us to waste them, so we never told her. We just trudged home with those big containers filled to the brim.

Our Mom was beside herself with joy when she got a good look at all those figs. She couldn't wait to get started washing and sorting them and piling them in an old enamel coated dishpan, where she completely covered them with sugar and left them overnight before she started cooking them.

There was usually more than one crop of figs a year, so when the time came for the second crop to come in, we'd find a bunch of excuses to call and talk to those neighbors or be seen playing around the big deep gully near their house, and if that didn't get the expected results we'd walk up and down the road whistling or singing or talking real loud. More times than not we were invited to come and gather those figs, but a few times they were generous enough to come and bring them to us. These were real gems for neighbors.

All in all, we'd wind up with all kinds of pickle jars and other odd glass containers filled with figs. They were not all sealed real well, but we ate them so rapidly they seldom had time to spoil.   The very last two or three jars had to be saved for Christmas breakfast, which was a tradition we kept going forever.

Our other favorite preserves was pear. We didn't have to hint around for those, we had this gigantic old pear tree that was probably brought over on the Mayflower, right in our backyard, and few were the years that it wasn't loaded. These pears were large, firm and juicy, just right for preserves!

They were nearly always too far up in the tree for us little kids to pick, but if we waited for them to fall the chickens and bees got to them before we did. The bees did little damage other than hiding themselves on the opposite side of the pears and pulling off a sneaky sting attack on us unsuspecting, victims.

Mostly we collected the pears by bumping the large limbs with a strong pole after which we'd run like a turkey trying to keep them from pelting us. If and when one hit us it really hurt, because they were so large and hard, walloping a pack of about a 10-pound rock as they fell down with great force. In spite of all our haste to dodge them we'd often get a big lump on our head or a black eye from them.

We loved to eat them between meals as a snack, but we had to be careful not to eat too many, as they had the same effect as a laxative. In preparation for the preserves we'd wash a whole bunch of them and sit down with a good sharp butcher knife to start peeling them. They had to be sliced from the stiff cores to a certain size in order for them to cook fast and make a pretty clear fruit spread when done. As we sliced them, we'd divide the little pieces out *equally* - two for preserves, one for the peeler!

Things went along really well till we peeled into one of those little skinny pink, super-energized worms; at which time our pace was slowed tremendously, as we watched much more carefully what we were slicing into.

The longer we peeled and sliced the sharper our knives got, and pretty soon first one and then the other peeler would hop up from his seat, plop his finger in his mouth and make a bee line for some cold water to stop the bleeding. Of course, with his finger all tied up with a white rag, his peeling time was cut down to about half.

When all the pears were prepared, our Mom would place them in that seasoned old dishpan coated with enamel, cover them with sugar, add a few slices of lemon and make a hot fire in the stove to start them cooking. She stirred them often, while us kids found some empty glass jars and washed them so they'd be ready when the preserves got done.

If our Mom was busy with something else while the pears cooked, she'd ask one of us to stir them so they wouldn't bum. We were more than happy to, as we plotted to sample them during this time.

Finally, they were the right color and consistency, so she'd proceed to dip them up and put them in the various and sundry type jars that we had found and readied for that purpose. We were all hanging over and around the process waiting for her to get those last few pieces out so we could dive into that pan and start sopping it out with our fingers.

When we had cleaned the pan thoroughly by sopping and washed all the excessive sticky off our face and fingers, we were sweetened up good enough to last at least till supper and felt happy to have so many preserves for all those cold morning breakfasts.

Spending The Night With Granny

When I was small, my Granny (on Dad's side) was very old. She was a small half-Creek Indian lady, who was very quiet and reserved. As a result of a fall many years ago she was left with a big hump on her back and could not stand up straight. My Grandpa, who was dead before I came along, had lost a leg in the Confederate Army. The only thing about him I ever saw was his wooden leg, and that was no prize to look at.

Granny's house was near ours, and for as long as I can remember, my Mother cooked her meals and sent them by kid, down the path to her house. Earlier on she had prepared her own breakfast and coffee. We trudged out quite a trail to her house; it went up and down and over and around and finally across a foot-plank to her yard.

All of the grass and weeds were kept worn off of this path; only vines, bushes and briars protruded on either side, which were a real nuisance when the dew or rain was on them.

For years, my older brothers and Father took turns spending the night with Granny, but on occasions she would walk all the way around the road to our house where she'd spend the night with us. She always stopped by the cemetery where her husband and two sons were buried, and spent a while pulling up weeds before she proceeded to our house with her sun bonnet on her head and her individual chamber pot under her arm. When all of the older fellars had other plans they would bribe or persuade one or two of us girls to spend the night with her. We weren't overjoyed at the thought, but when we remembered her home-baked gingersnaps or hoop cheese, the idea was much more enticing.

As soon as the sun began to set we'd get Granny's supper and hop off down the path, ready to spend the night.

Poor Granny had nothing for entertainment, so we were conditioned for a dull evening. In warm weather we sat on her small porch watching any and everything that moved. As we sat there we'd scare the chickens off the steps or catch lightning bugs or smack mosquitoes. Sometimes she'd have the items to make a "hummer button" on a string, which we would sit and wind up for a long time, or we'd do string tricks on our hands (Jacob's ladder, crow's feet, etc.) or pick up five smooth stones to play Jack Stones with. If we put our heads together we could usually find something to help us pass the time.

At the edge of her porch was a persimmon tree over which we kept close watch. We wanted to be sure we beat the 'possums to the ripe ones which fell off as soon as they were ripe. One evening our little brother decided to pull a trick on his younger sister, so he pulled one of the persimmons and pretended to take a bite, after which he offered the sister a bite. She was too young to know you didn't *pull* persimmons off the tree, so she bit down on it amazed at the drawing pull it left in her mouth. This rough, shriveled feeling always stayed in your mouth for a long time. The poor little girl was frenzied as the impish little brother giggled. She had definitely learned her lesson about the persimmons.

Granny's house was a real old one, built in two sections, as a lot of them were back then. The main part consisted of her bedroom, which also sufficed for her living room, and a back bedroom (much older) with open windows that had shutters to close them. This room had no ceiling, so she used those exposed 2 X 4's that ran horizontally, to set her canned foods on. This room was also used for all other storage, including chicken feed. This room was where everyone spending the night had to sleep.

We girls were really afraid to go to sleep with the windows open, and it was too hot and stuffy with them closed. Any little noise we heard was definitely a monster of some sort. Mouse traps were a common sight as the chicken feed was a drawing card for mice. If and when one of them snapped, we'd almost jump out of bed. Before the night was over we firmly decided that we would not come back to spend the night any time soon, emergency or not.

When it began to get light, Granny would bail out of bed, dress completely, and make a start for the kitchen. Her kitchen was a separate room that was connected to the other part of the house by a little open breezeway, which was where she kept her wash pan and bucket of water with a dipper in it. In this little pan she washed her face and hands and dried them with a little towel that hung on a nail close by. From here she opened the kitchen door, taking her water bucket with her.

First she made a fire in her small cook stove and got the coffee going. You could smell that strong Luzianne coffee a couple of miles away. We kids didn't drink it but she did, all day long!! She never threw any leftover coffee away, she just heated it up and drank every drop of it. Her old enamel covered tall coffee pot had no strainer, so all of the grounds settled in the bottom of the pot, making the last cup or two awfully strong.

As soon as she had the coffee going, she would make up several biscuits and maybe fry an egg or two. Just as we had hoped, she had some of that good soft hoop cheese to eat with those hot biscuits and blackstrap (unsulphured molasses). We did enjoy our breakfast!

When we had finished eating we got a couple of little buckets and went to the spring to get her daily supply of water. We usually did her laundry at our house, so she didn't use very much water. With the water chore behind us we'd gather the eggs and help feed her few chickens before we left.

One of our brothers had seen a chicken snake in her little chicken house that swallowed a whole egg as he watched, so we were extremely cautious about getting in and out of that little house. There were very few eggs to gather but everyone took special care to find and gather all of their eggs, since they could be used like cash at the store. It seemed like Granny always had an old hen "setting" hatching baby chickens, and they were awfully grouchy, often pecking at you if you got too close, making that job one to be glad to be over with.

By this time of day the sun was up and getting warm, and we were ready to head for home, where we hoped we could take a nap sometime during the day. But just as we started to leave, Granny would decide one of us should trim her toenails or rub her back with liniment.

When we finally started up the path toward our house we could hear her batting at the chickens on the porch as she hollered "shoooooo!" and continued sweeping her little porch, not because it needed it but because it gave her something to do.

Gathering Mule Feed (Fodder)

When the corn had matured and the blades (fodder) on the stalks began to turn brownish, it meant the "fodder" pulling season was upon us. There were large fields and long rows of corn all over the fields in our area, and the fodder from the stalks was the staple food for mules and horses during the winter months. Grass was not grown the year round when I was a kid, so hay and fodder, and other provisions for animals were a must.

No one looked forward to these hot, menial, physically demanding tasks, but everyone made time for the gathering of these crops which were essential to their animals' well being.

Our household was blessed with a lot of strong healthy men who always handled that job for us, but some of the other households were not so lucky. Sometimes the women had to help out in the cases where there was a manpower shortage. The work was not so heavy, but was strenuous and tiring.

Day after day our brothers and father stripped the corn stalks from daylight till dark, trying to save all the animal feed they could before it was ruined by too much rain. The blades were collected and held in both hands till there was no more room and then they were placed together under one arm while the other hand took a few blades and wrapped around the small bundle called a "hand" and tied it so as to hold the blades together. These little bundles were about eight to ten inches in diameter and were placed on a broken over cornstalk to dry in the sun.

When a lot of bundles had accumulated and were sufficiently dried, the children were rounded up and brought to the field in the wagon to gather them and pile them on the wagon to be carried to the barn. After a lot of passing the bundles from the cornstalks to the wagon, we'd have a load, so we'd crawl up on top and ride to the barn where we'd proceed to unload it all and fling it up to a "catcher" standing in the barn loft. Each end of the loft was open so it was easier to pitch the fodder up (or down). The only hitch was the catcher would miss a few bundles and we'd have to re-pitch them. We thought that was funny, so we'd really clown around with those bundles.

As soon as that load was stored in the barn we'd start back to the field to get another load, but enroute we'd draw a fresh bucket of water and take to the men. They always welcomed a cool drink and a little resting period. The weather was very hot at this time of year, and those dry, crisp leaves were very scratchy often leaving little scratched marks everywhere they touched your skin.

When mother nature saw fit, she'd make it possible for a few later watermelons to be ripe near one of the corn fields, where all the fodder-pulling activity was. This was a much anticipated pleasure that we couldn't wait to indulge in. With all eyes focused on the watermelon seekers, it wasn't hard to tell if our treats were available. The little melons were lop-sided, with a lighter spot on the underside. We judged if it were ripe by the little vine at one end where the melon was connected to the main plant.

We'd yank one of the little ones off the vine and smash it with our fist to see if it was red on the inside. When we saw the ripe sweet meat we were ecstatic with joy. It didn't take long for us to snatch up several of the small melons to take back to where the men folks were. After wiping our hands on our dresses and overalls, we busted them all open and dug in with our hands, digging all of the edible red meat out - boy howdy! That was good stuff! The juice dripping off our elbows was soon wiped off on our clothes as we proceeded to fight duels with the tiny slippery seeds.

Soon, someone would call off the games and we'd all go back to our respective jobs. If a rain was approaching, everyone would join in and just load the dried fodder bundles on the wagon and try to get it to the barn before it got soaked. We didn't mind a little rain falling on us; it was nice to get cooled off, but the fodder would mold and ruin if it got wet.

When the sun came out again the same procedure was followed till all the best cornstalks had been stripped. Unfortunately, on some of the blades were those funny looking stinging creatures called "pack saddles" and we were awfully apprehensive about just grabbing those blades without looking real good. Don't know why they called them pack saddles, but I guess it was derived from the mean sting they "packed" when they got a chance. Very seldom did we get the whole crop in before someone got stung by one of the little devils.

A few times when bad weather was coming in, or the weekend approaching, we'd be forced to haul fodder into the night hours by the moonlight. That was kinda fun cause it was a lot cooler at night, and after the dew hit the fodder it wasn't nearly as scratchy.

As soon as all the fodder had been stripped and stored, we'd find all kinds of excuses to climb up in the barn loft to play in it and even jump out of the barn loft to see if we could land on our feet. Some of the more stupid kids in our area came up with the idea of taking bundles of fodder in each arm and flapping them like a bird flaps its wings, thinking they could fly. Luckily the soft hay or grass on the ground beneath furnished a pretty good cushion, keeping them from getting hurt, but they sure learned they couldn't fly that way!

At any rate, there was real cause for rejoicing when we finished that job each year, and there was a lot of satisfaction in knowing our beasts of burden would be fed through the winter.

Revolutionary Basket Weaving

The home demonstration agent's popularity soared to its greatest height when this new craft came to town. She would have been the top contender for the Nobel prize or Oscar or top discovery of the year! Nothing ever took our community by storm to such degree.

As soon as the word about those magnificent baskets got around, the usual three or four attendees at the Home Demonstration Club swelled to "nowhere to sit capacity." The attention at these meetings was like 150 per cent, and everyone busied themselves with finding honey-suckle vines, which was no problem in our area up until this time. That vine was the #1 pestilence plant till the arrival of the kudzu vine.

The procedure for priming those vines for use involved pulling or cutting the longest length vines you could get, stripping off all the greenery and little suckers growing on either side, and then skinning off the thin brownish top layer of covering, as you readied the vines to be soaked in a big tub of water. These were soaked overnight to make them more limber, or pliable, and easier to finish cleaning.

If you were a fast learner and caught on to all the instructions the agent gave you at the last meeting, you could rig up a wooden bottom and start weaving the vines right around it, tacking the vines on at intervals to make them stay in place, using the firm, flat surface for a base. Then you were ready to really get down to business weaving and criss-crossing the vines to whatever size your heart desired. But, on the other hand, not everyone was quite so astute! Some slow learners had to take their vines in hand and go to their neighbor's house to be reinstructed in the art.

As a last resort, they would even imitate the same facial expressions of their teacher and all but sit on her lap to get the right slant on the vine handling. If you sat across the room from the instructor it all looked backward, and occasionally someone would start off trying to maneuver the vines backward, after which they would have to unwind and start over time and again.

Most of the learners had to be instructed over and over to perfect the technique. There were all kinds of baskets to be made, but the most cherished and widely used pattern was the tall flower holder with a wide brim around the top and a tall, thin handle that stood up over the whole thing. The flower container was set about eight inches down into the body of the basket. The size was perfect for a quart fruit jar, which was nearly always what wound up holding the flowers.

The really ingenious weavers would create new sizes and shapes for those wonder baskets. Some looked like bread servers, while some looked like decorative sewing baskets, and a lot of them looked like the dickens, but mostly they were short, middle-sized or tall flower baskets with those over-sized handles standing straight up serving no purpose at all.

Where there was more than one grown-up girl in the family, there would be two or three workers sitting close together with a bale of those vines strewn all around just a-winding and twisting the strands as they sang some of those good old hymns such as "'P'air in tha Blud" or "Whut er Fren we have in Geeeezus," or "Intha Sweeeet By'n By" while enjoying themselves immensely.

Most of the finished products would not stand close inspection, but it was a new industry without a market that had no cash involved, and everyone was doing it at their own pace and in their own way, all the while getting a big kick out of it.

The whole procedure demanded some concentration and was time consuming and scratchy. Those little sharp ends had to be concealed, giving the impression of one continuous "earth long" vine being used per basket

Some of our closest neighbors were really masters of the art. They made beautiful, perfectly proportioned baskets and even painted them! They chose light green or white paint as a rule, which turned out to be the officially accepted color for everyone's baskets. Many of them were used at our church when the prettiest flowers were in full bloom, lending a cheerful color to the otherwise drab and sad-looking sanctuary. Several of the neighbors wanted to swap baskets with them or trade off some other item they had on hand, but instead these generous friends would give them one for birthdays, wedding presents, or Christmas gifts. It was not long before this new fad had spread all over creation.

Everywhere you went they had some of those baskets on display or were busy making one. Every house, and often every room, had one or two in them with some on the porches.

If this craze had not come along, the erosion in our area might have been curbed before the introduction of kudzu. We really stripped off all those vines we could get to in our wild frenzies to create a bunch of those baskets. We didn't even think about how those vines had previously helped to hold the soil back. We were just interested in creating a little beauty without any thought of the devastation that would follow.

Checkers And Set Back Experts

Mostly in the winter months, when farming was at a standstill, or put on hold, the local men would congregate at the local store, claim a seat near the big heater, pull up a table of sorts, and engage a playing force of four for set-back, or talk some willing partner into a fierce game of checkers. Most of these men had come prepared for the occasion, complete with overalls and their preference of tobacco.

The store-keepers kept sand-filled cans placed at strategic points for all the tobacco chewers and cigarette butts of the heavy smokers. The average group consisted of the usual game players, overseers, and a few non-committeds.

Many of these older men were seasoned players, and they knew all the rules and ins and outs of the games. A few of them were very proficient, a lot of them inefficient, but that's why the games held so much fascination for them.

The real eager beavers made a point to get to the store early so they could be included in the first round of games. Several of the congregated came just to observe and maybe help their favorites out just a little in a pinch. No one ever had that accusing finger pointed at him, but from time to time hints were thrown out to let everyone know a little hanky-panky might be going on. All of those ear-flippings and throat-clearings weren't accidental.

As soon as the cards had been dealt, a great quiet surrounded the place. If a spectator opened his mouth he was quickly quieted down. The only noise at this time was the frequent customers who had run out of some staple item at home and were forced to come to the store for it. If they were women, they'd glance over toward the game group with a disdainful look and march right on back home as soon as their mission was accomplished.

After much head scratching and complaining about the "sorry hands" they'd drawn, a bid was settled on, unneeded cards discarded and needed ones dealt to those who needed them, and this is when the real concentration began. At this time the "watch crew" was set in motion; they'd ease around behind all the players, often trying to give advice on how to play the cards and occasionally sneezing all over somebody's hand, after which they'd yank out that ole blue bandana hanky and start wiping off all the sprayed surfaces and then blowing their nose real hard for an encore.

The players could watch these guys' expressions and see what kind of cards their opponents had, but not for long, most of the players held their cards real close to their bodies or face down on the table. It was not uncommon for one of the players to look at the other fellar's cards pretending he thought they were his, and at every opportunity they'd peep over at the other fellars' hands trying to see what was there. Once they got underway, these games would go on and on. The losers refused to give up their seats to let the winners play some other eager beavers, and often a tie would evolve, which helped to prolong the sessions.

When mealtime came, if the husbands had not come home, the wives would often send one of the kids to the store to tell their daddy, "Dinner's ready." The standard reply was, "Go on home son, tell your mama I'll be home in a minute." (which was an afternoon long). Mostly the players were so wound up with winning or losing, they'd just buy a "3-centa" (cola) and some sardines or pork 'n beans and crackers and just eat right there on the scene.

A few of the onlookers went home for dinner and a quick nap, after which they'd hurry back to see what the status was among the card players and checker games. No one ever thought of leaving till it began to get dark, at which time they had to hurry home to slop the hogs and feed the other farm animals. The store's closing was the only thing that roused some of them out.

The checkers players were the real thinkers and slow movers. They'd do trial moves and imaginary plays before they'd do anything permanent, making the same game go on for hours. If one man had lost several games, and it looked like he was gonna lose another, he'd "accidentally" knock the board, or one of his close friends would stand up and move the board just enough to dislocate the checkers, then everyone's temper would flare up as they stirred around with all kinds of accusations.

A few of the "short-fused" men would have to go outside to settle their differences, just short of a fist fight. These were usually the ones who had small wagers on someone special's winning. They all knew almost everyone would do a little cheating in a tight spot but they were so interested in that "pastime" they never mentioned it. Anyway, it would have been a case of the pot calling the kettle black, and when they started disqualifying all of the guilty ones, there would have been none left to play (just like in the local and federal governments).

Learning The "Two-Step"

You don't realize what a real frustrating problem is till you tackle learning the "two-step" by "The Fate of Floyd Collins" or "Letter Edged in Black!"? These were records that we owned and played relentlessly on our graphaphone (record player). Of course, only the girls would tackle such a wild undertaking as the two-step, but someone had witnessed other people doing it, and we needed to learn it if we were gonna keep up with the times.

The fellars weren't at all interested in improving their dancing skills, so we girls had to couple up and improvise as we tried that daresome new dance.

It was really exasperating trying to figure out who was leading, At times both of us were, but it really didn't matter, we were each dancing to a different tempo (whatever that was). Our large, bare feet were none too nimble in the first place, and our lack of instructions did not qualify us for a "twinkle toes" trophy. The best thing about the whole thing was we didn't have to be too quick nor exert too much energy in the effort to keep time with the music.

When we cranked up the old graphaphone and placed the needle cap down on the record we had to listen closely to tell when the music started up. The scratching from the old worn out needle was real disturbing, to the point of making your flesh "crawl," and the regular tone from the record was so high pitched it was kinda nauseating, but that record player freed up a dance partner for one of us girls, so we always tried it first. If the scratchy needle was so bad we couldn't tell when to start stepping, one of the older girls would start banging away on the upright piano, which was also out of tune. That left one girl without a partner, but it didn't really matter, we'd just dance by ourselves.

227

The tunes the piano player knew, other than hymns, weren't too lively either. Some of them, such as "Jeannie with Her Light Brown Hair," "Home on the Range," and "Birmingham Jail" were so slow we'd actually wobble in between steps, but no one was judging so we just enjoyed ourselves.

There were no screen doors around at this time, so it was common for one of our old hound dogs to sneak in and hide behind the piano or sofa when no one was looking, but as soon as that old piano got going real loud and choppy, he'd hop out and make a fast get-a-way or go into a "running fit" and scare the daylights out of us.

That broke up our dance sessions, pronto. It took us all to run the dog out of the room and it also took all of the joy out of the dancing lessons. Them dancing lessons were definitely put on hold till another time when everything had quieted down and we had our field chores caught up with.

The only dancing we ever did away from home was square dancing, so there was no real reason to know how to "two-step", nor fox trot, nor the Charleston. It was just a little something different for us to try. But, with all of this expertise we'd just acquired we were awfully eager to try out that slow two-step every chance we got. When the music makers at the square dances started doodling around with a new tune in between dances, we'd hop out on the dance floor and strut our stuff. The older onlookers seemed to like these different, slower renditions. Guess they thought they might be able to handle that step themselves at one time or another.

At nearly all of the Saturday night square dances there was this particular older man who loved to attend them; he never square danced, but in between sessions, he'd brush up on his "buck and wing" dance. He was really a good dancer, and when he started dancing everyone watched as the older spectators started clapping their hands and patting their feet in rhythm. He also commented on his approval of the new two-step, which gave us a lot of confidence.

228

Scarecrow

You didn't plant scarecrows like a seed when you planted your watermelon seed. It took a lot of imagination, ingenuity, and some real expertise to come up with a good one. The location was a major factor, they had to be in the best and most visible spots to be most effective. Even if scarecrows did not serve a useful purpose they were interesting and entertaining. We always watched for them as we passed the fields or patches wherever we went. Almost every farmer had one or two placed at strategic places in his crop fields and patches.

With the crow population at an all time high and the other birds feeling free to help themselves to anything they could dig their beaks into, these little people look-alikes were the best things the farmers knew to do to try to scare them off.

Scarecrows were not the easiest things in the world to make. You had to be pretty ingenious to come up with one that could really hold up during all kinds of weather. It took good lumber and strong nails for the frame, with a lot 'of padding to produce a body-like form. All of the clothes, faces, and hats were strictly the products of a good imagination and artistic ability. Each one had its own personality, with "designer" clothes and finishing touches.

The outerwear, which was all that showed, had to be sturdy garb that someone had outgrown or discarded for one reason or another. Their faces were painstakingly concocted to resemble a real person, even with hats or caps on and maybe a pipe in his mouth. Some of them had empty buckets on their arms or brooms in their hands for a more real life appearance.

Intentional or not, each farmer's scarecrow was different. Their clothes, their faces, the way they were turned, their sizes and even the way they were proportioned. It was as though the farmers were competing for the best scarecrow. I really think they enjoyed putting one together for the whole neighborhood to see and pass judgment on. I kinda expect they had names for them, since they were around so much of the time and so much was expected of them.

If their hat disappeared, it had to be replaced, if their clothes got too tattered, they had to be re-dressed, if the frames got warped or fell over, they certainly had to be re-worked, always with the idea of making a more clever one than before. Most of the time it was a family project incorporating everyone's ideas so as to give it more individuality.

No one ever determined whether the scarecrows really warded off the crows and other bird culprits, or If they just occupied the space and drew attention. Either way they were definitely a tradition and usually, after stormy weather, we hurried out to see if the scarecrow was still intact. With a little imagination and a lot of admiration one could easily compose a little song poem about them. This is one I thought up:

Funny little scarecrow, scarecrow, scarecrow
dressed up like a silly clown
but has no place to go.
With his tattered straw hat
and his faded raggedy shirt
standing in the rain and sun
keeping out the crows.
Smiling whether tired or not
looking pleased with what he's got
watching watermelons grow
getting not a bite.
Busy little scarecrow, scarecrow, scarecrow
doesn't wave to anyone
has to help things grow
at attention on his job
no one ever sees him sob.
Never takes the time to nap
has to watch for crows
busy earning all his keep

230

while some others try to sleep
can't see anything he does
as the hours drag by.
Sissy little scarecrow, scarecrow, scarecrow
acting like a real tough guy
scaring off the crows.
Swaying gently in the breeze
watching birds build in the trees
telling nothing, seeing all
what a way to be!
Shaking quietly in the dark
when a little dog would bark
if a crow should peck him
little would he know.

A Squirrel Hunt

To go squirrel hunting meant just that. It was not just to see if you could find a cute little squirrel and watch him running in and out of his nest as he leaped from one tree to another, shaking his bushy little tail.

No sireeee, squirrel was a cherished meat that was enjoyed by one and all. The young squirrels were fried and the older ones wound up in dumplings. It also meant that several cartridges or shells would be used, and those were precious.

Having inherited a great love for the outdoors and almost as big a love for hunting and fishing, most of our men were very good "shots" and pretty good hunters (a little of the Creek coming through).

A couple of our older brothers prided themselves in training bird dogs and fox hounds and were very good at those sports themselves. Being excellent marksmen, when they went bird hunting you could count the shells they took with them and nearly always depend on that many birds for supper. A wasted shell was not tolerated.

One day one of the older brothers decided to take our youngest brother (who was a lot younger) squirrel hunting with him to teach him all the tricks of the trade. They both found their overall jackets, got a cap and found a few shells for their particular guns and .were all set to blast off, except for a pocket full of peanuts or pecans, which were a vital part of the ritual.

The younger brother was limited to a .22 rifle, while the older one shouldered a genuine shotgun. They really looked more like father and son as they trudged off down a path in the cow pasture, heading for the hunting grounds.

Squirrels were not plentiful around there as all the farmers kept them thinned out for food. So this excursion took them quite a long trek from home. The trees were plentiful and the undergrowth thick. When you were in the deep forest you didn't travel fast for all the briars and limbs flapping you in the face and the rotten logs and sticks breaking underfoot. Also you needed to watch for snakes or any other animal you might happen up on.

Around the marshy places my older brother was always on the alert for signs of mink or muskrat, or even foxes. He, along with the other brothers, were avid trappers, and during the course of a winter sold several furs from the animals they trapped.

At some point the fellars got separated. which was a grave mistake, since the younger brother had not been versed in finding his way home or out of the woods. He must have wandered around a long time before realizing he was lost. It seems the older brother got carried away looking for a squirrel nest or a mink track and lost track of time. When he looked around and listened and could not hear nor see anyone he proceeded to call for his hunting partner. The younger one didn't hear anything but the crackling sticks and leaves he was stepping on, so he proceeded to travel on in his mad search for a squirrel.

A lot of time elapsed, and I'm sure a lot of anxious minutes went by, not to mention the frustration the older brother felt for letting the younger one out of his sight.

They both ambled around hunting each other and yelling to the top of their lungs without getting an inkling of a reply. It was impossible to track anyone on that heavy leaf-covered ground, only a few broken down briars would have been clues for directions used.

As the afternoon wore on it began to get a little dark in the woods, and I'm sure both fellars began to panic. The younger one was probably scared out of his wits, with the darkened forest closing in on him, and a few birds making their weird calls. His imagination must have been working overtime wondering what might jump out from behind some of those trees.

As luck would have it, the younger one somehow found a clearing and ultimately a road, so he just made a bee-line for home, to the bewilderment of the home folks. He tried to describe his plight and explain why he'd come on back, while out in the woods the older guy dreaded to return home without the lil' brother.

Eventually, the older one was seen coming through the pasture looking terribly worried. Several of us ran to meet him and tell him the younger brother was already home, safe and sound.

That was the best possible news he could have heard as he let out a big whoop. He tried to justify their separation, but ultimately it all turned out to be an amusing tale that was related time and again. We even made up a song about the older brother spending most of his hunting time hunting his little lost brother.

Setting A Rabbit Box ("Gums")

In the fall when all the baby rabbits had grown up to about half-grown, all of the farmers loved to eat the tender fellars, and we used all kinds of methods to try to snare them, other than shooting them. Probably the best way was catching them in those famous rabbit boxes or "gums" as they were commonly called.

Every household out in the country had at least one such box. They were little long rectangular wooden boxes about 2x2 feet long, eight inches high and approximately six inches wide. They were built with a trap lid that closed when anything touched the trigger. Of course you had to use the proper bait (mostly apples and cabbage leaves) and set the trap where you had located a frequently used rabbit trail, recognized by the little round pellets scattered around.

When someone at the community store sold one of those prized rabbits it really created a chain reaction amongst the other locals. They could realistically envision all that cash they could rake in with a few of those young rabbits, as they busied themselves repairing and cleaning up their old rabbit gums.

With these boxes positioned just right and the baited trap all set, they'd hurry off to get out of sight in case some little half-starved rabbit came hopping by and wanted to investigate the new apparatus that was occupying that place in his trail.

As soon as morning came someone would make haste to check out the rabbit box. The trap would not always be sprung, but when it was, great care was utilized in opening the door. On a few occasions a skunk had been trapped. However, you could usually tell that before you got there, and that presented a real problem. You certainly didn't want that odor on your hands, and at best you had to wash and wash and try to fumigate the box before it could be re-used, if ever.

It wasn't unusual to open up the trap door to see the long, sharp, ugly nose of a 'possum occupying the box. Your first impulse was to stomp the scalawag for messing up your chances to catch a rabbit, but after re-thinking the matter for a few seconds, you came up with the idea of someone's likelihood of wanting him to eat. So you carried the 'possum, box and all, home and caged up the ugly ole critter to fatten and either ate it yourself or gave it to someone else to eat. When our Mom cooked one our Dad was about the only one who could stomach it, but the dogs enjoyed it. With those boxes set you were indeed lucky if you didn't catch some neighbor's half-wild cat. If and when you did, the second you opened the trap door, the scared cat jumped right straight up in your face, climbed and clawed down your clothes to the ground and ran away like he'd been shot out of a cannon.

Those things being the exceptions, you did catch a rabbit more times than not, and the sight of a little scared, big-eared, wide-eyed rabbit really created a bunch of excitement for the whole family. As soon as the little rabbit had been stored away safely till his fate was decided, someone would hurry back to the rabbit gum and reset the trap, hoping to catch another one overnight.

In the meantime, the one that was caught was killed and half-way cleaned to be taken to the store where they hoped someone would buy him for a dime. If it didn't sell, they just brought him on back home, finished cleaning him, and our Mother fried him up for supper, made some good thickened gravy and hot biscuits, and enjoyed the change of tenure for a delicious supper.

236

Hiding The Booze Bottles

In depression days, bootleggers were a dime a dozen. In nearly all them large, back-woodsy, untraveled (by the public) areas, one could invariably find either a working whiskey still or where one had been in operation. It was illegal to make and sell "moonshine" or "popskull" or "white lightning," but the penalties if caught were so lenient the bootleggers weren't very concerned about it.

There were a few exceptions when a new sheriff took office and was obligated to fulfill his campaign promises to wage war on the bootleggers. At these times (before the sheriff got bought off by the big whiskey makers), shooting confrontations erupted and a few still watchers were killed.

This illegal booze was very potent but a lot cheaper than the store-bought brands. With a lot of Baptists around, the church goers were condemned, if not put out of the church, for getting drunk and creating a disturbance after drinking the stuff.

If one of the men in our community had gone without booze for a while and had serious notions about quitting drinking, some of his friends (??) or hunting buddies would invite him to go on a coon or fox hunt, and before he got home his will power had lost its strength.

There were no women in our neighborhood who drank whiskey, to my knowledge, and almost all of them despised it with a passion. The strong drink literally stank, and the men didn't just take a drink, they drank until they were totally and disgustingly inebriated. Our Dad belonged to that group. We enjoyed his wit and knowledge when he was sober, but we grew to despise him when he was hopelessly drunk.

It appeared that any father of three or four teenage boys would know there was no such thing as hiding a liquor bottle or jar around his house, but our Dad insisted on trying. We learned from our friends that this was a common practice at their house too. Guess the men thought if they sneaked out behind the barn and took a "nip" their wives wouldn't know about it.

With boys being boys, it didn't take them long to figure out what was going on, so they made a habit of watching their dads as they came home. At one glance they could tell if he'd been drinking, so they sneaked around and watched him to see where he hid his bottle. At first, they would just find it and smell of it and then they would rehide it or pour a little of it out, and I expect they also tasted it to see what it tasted like, if they could swallow it.

When the boys got with their friends they'd often discuss how they found the hiding places and exchange tales about how they'd sometimes have to boost each other up to feel around on top of the ledges in the outhouses. If the bottle was accidentally knocked off and busted all over the floor, they'd "high tail" it out from there lest they be seen leaving the scene of the crime. Then, too, there was the chance of getting cut on the glass, which would identify the culprit who would have surely been punished unmercifully.

After a couple of weeks of a drunk Dad, the older fellars at our house would dilute the booze, not realizing our Dad would know the difference. It must have worked a real hardship on our Dad always trying to find a new hiding place. He'd even come in after dark so the boys couldn't see where he hid it. We were all so disgusted at his staggering around, his loudness and even meanness, that one of my brothers just plain urinated in a half empty bottle. Don't know for sure how our Dad found out about it, but there wasn't a whole lot he could say, especially when he didn't know for sure who did it.

Whenever us kids would wander around in the edges of the pasture or woods we were always running into discarded fruit jars. Most of them smelled like whiskey, but had been drained; but every now and then we'd find one that had a few drops left in it. We didn't dare taste it cause our Mom could have smelled it before we got in

238

the house and would have "worn us out" (switched our legs).

If we found as much as a couple of spoonfuls in one of the discarded fruit jars, we would test it on some unsuspecting ants coming out of their anthills, or if we saw a caterpillar, he would be the target. We loved to see them squirm and then die. One ole man "'lowed as how" it would keep you from having stomach worms if you drank a little all along. The best use we found for whiskey, and the only reason it was permitted in our house was to be poured over camphor gum to make a medication that we used for a lot of things (external, of course).

Quilting Techniques

When the weather was rainy or cold our Mom entertained herself with quilting. The top priority was sewing clothes for the whole clan, but she was a fast worker and handled that chore with great speed. All of the left-over scraps from our dresses were saved to be used for making those little squares which she put together for quilt tops of varying patterns.

This ritual was a wide spread practice and sooner or later some awards were won when the best of these "pride and joy" jobs were put on display. Some of them were also sold for extra spending money. Everyone in the community was anxious to see everyone else's creations, partly so they could copy the other fellars ideas for designs.

Some of the quilts were lovely, some of them unusual, some of them of good quality and some of them just practical warm covers. If my Mom ever saw a pattern (there must have been a blue million) she'd ask for it or make herself one very similar. Hers were all made from little fragments of material (mostly figured) cut out of various bits of cloth and sewed together by hand to make a square about 12" to 14". It took a long time to make enough squares for even a skimpy bed cover. Us kids were real inquisitive about the new squares, we wanted to see how many pieces like our dresses we could identify. We spent long periods looking them all over and deciding who had a dress like each piece.

Many days we'd come home from school on a dreary day, in a bad mood and starved to death, only to find our Mom sitting all hunkered over with a lap full of messy fabric pieces all engrossed in her quilt top. We knew she hadn't cooked anything special for us to munch on when we came home from school so this made us despise the project even more. She'd even slave over those little jibbles of cloth and be late cooking supper, an unpardonable sin, for Dad and us.

After weeks of preparation she'd get all those squares finished and then she'd start "carding the bats." This looked like more fun and she'd let us help her with that. It was accomplished with two wood paddles which had metal bristles on the insides. The cotton for the quilt filler was scraped across the bristles over and over till it was very smooth and thin. Then it was removed and piled in a special place till there were enough to cover a bed. We only had double beds which were bought with the intentions of letting two or three kids sleep together on them.

When all the cotton bats were ready we'd have to get out the quilting frames. These were four 7 to 9 foot long poles with holes drilled all along to adjust them as the quilting progressed. Along with these long poles was stored 4 extra long nails to place in the holes to keep the poles in place after the quilt had been stitched to them sufficiently. At this point this huge frame was placed on top of four chairs spaced the full size of the frames apart. Some of our neighbors hung their frames from the ceiling but Mom found them easier to handle on the chair tops.

There were no extra rooms in our house so we used the "boys" room to set up operations. At the sight of this monstrosity covering their whole room the boys flew into a rage but were soon quieted down with the sight of a green "hickory." During this quilting thing they had to crawl under, skinny around or step on their beds to get from one place to another in their room. Their room had been selected because of the good light from the windows and there was never as much activity in there as there was in the other rooms, including our Mother's room.

We had a wide long hall but it wasn't quite the right dimensions to accommodate everything that was needed for that job. All of the girls who could handle and thread a needle got in on the fun?! Only our Mom could sew with a thimble on her finger so the rest of us got stuck with pricked fingers from start to finish. By the time we got a plain bottom lining, added the cotton bats and placed the pieced squares for the top together, the quilt was kind of thick in places and was hard for the needle to penetrate at the seams, but we kept hacking away at it 'til we had a whole "round" finished, then we'd roll the quilt up on two sides and started stitching big swirls on another round.

When all the material had been properly stitched and rolled up we'd be ready to unroll it and bind it all around with a blending solid colored material. When finished, it was something to be proud of blue ribbon quality or not. Some homes had quilting parties where the available women met and quilted all day or evening. They were held mostly in homes where there weren't many helpers. We didn't need one and I don't remember that our Mom ever went to one. It was all we could do to keep enough cover for all our own beds and have some to give to the older kids as they got married off and set up housekeeping.

Some of the time as soon as we'd get one quilt finished we'd start saving little material pieces to make another top, only with a different pattern.

Doomed Birds Of A Feather

On our farm there was no lack of birds. Big birds, little birds, good birds, bad birds, song birds and pretty birds. They all had a purpose I'm sure, and some of them were to irritate me. For instance, there was this noisy mocking bird that couldn't be discouraged from going completely through his long repertoire of songs every day just after lunch. His stage was the tall cedar tree right by the corner of our front porch. His main and most appreciative audience was my mother. This was her nap or rest period and her bedroom window was very close by.

Instead of a nap I chose to draw and paint on the porch and that particular bird irritated me, to no end. His singing was so unpredictable; one day he'd start off in the middle of his song, the next day he'd start at the end and work his way up and the next day he'd just sing at random. Whoever composed his music was tone deaf to say the least and I'd heard it so many times I was good and sick of it, so I decided to scare him off. One day I sneaked into the house and got the "ever-ready" 22 rifle, put a cartridge in it and slipped back out to the porch and tried to locate where the sound was coming from. The sun was very bright at that time of day and I couldn't look straight up for very long so I just shot at random, when suddenly the song was cut short with a small thud on the ground. Well, that was good riddance I figured till my Mom raised up and yelled "who shot my bird?" She didn't get a reply cause there was no need.

Even though they were not in such abundance in our area, we did have and could see the beautiful red cardinals the year round. These were more commonly known as "Red Birds" in our area. We were overjoyed to see one and made sure everyone else saw it so we could all make a wish, blow a kiss toward the bird for him to do his magic and make our wishes come true.

There were a lot of ever-searching big black buzzards. When we saw them we knew something had died so we watched them circling around and wondered what had died. These vultures or buzzards soared through the air with the greatest of ease and were halted only by a scent picked up by their peculiar noses which were equipped with an empty passageway just above their beaks.

They were always a mysterious lot as we could never get up real close to them whenever they were on the ground it was to clean up an old dead varmint of some kind. In a way they performed a good service and it's a shame they aren't more abundant today to help clean up the sides of the road. Our present day sanitation departments aren't nearly so dependable.

We had an enormous oak tree that stood just outside our cemetery fence and for some reason or other at least one buzzard could be seen parked on one of the upper branches a lot of the time. Guess this was a good observation point.

Since we had always wondered how they looked close up this was a great temptation to bring one down so we could inspect him. Well, I was the one who loved to shoot the rifle and since this was within my range I took it upon myself. When the big old ugly fellow hit the ground we all made a bee line to look him over and then hide him in a deep ditch. His nasty putrid appearance was even worse than we thought. It sure didn't take us long to see all we wanted to see. That certainly cured our curiosity about the buzzards.

There were all kinds of superstitions in our community; one of the most weird being the one about the screech owls. Since there were large forested areas back then, there was a big supply of these "bad-omen" birds, along with a lot of their cousins, the hoot owls and barn owls. Most nights in the spring or fall they loved to hear themselves alarming the whole neighborhood with their loud distinctive voices. If we weren't sleeping too good anyway, we'd listen to them and try to figure out which tree they were in. Sometimes they'd be real close to our house. We weren't too concerned except when a "screech owl" started to make his eerie noise. This meant bad news, maybe even someone close to you was gonna die. Being greatly disturbed by this warning we'd even be good to each other for days or even weeks till we heard of someone dying, which kinda broke the spell. We also believed a cock crowing at an unusual time meant sadness.

These and a million other superstitions were handed down from generation to generation and believed to be as true as the gospels. Bluebirds we never had many of because of our half-fed cats that always roamed around the out-houses, pastures and fields but we were truly cursed with those unwelcomed blue jays, thrashers, etc. One breed of birds our Dad tried to entice to our yard was Purple Martins. We erected a tall pole with gourds hung horizontally about four or five to a cross pole, with at least three cross poles so they could house a whole bunch of martins. They were not especially pretty except at some angles when the sun hit them and cast a purplish glint. The main reason for having them was to scare off chicken hawks.

Our martin gourds were positioned directly above our stove wood pile and I had made a real enemy out of some of them. They were kinda vicious little boogers and I'd throw at them as they dived down too close to my head. I seemed to be their only foe. They never let me gather wood without harassing me. One day ole vengeful me got out the rifle and loaded it (one shot) and as soon as I got my Dad out of sight I took real good aim and killed one of them. After all the shaming I got from my sisters, I picked him up and flung him across the pasture. Much to my amazement and horror my Dad found him in a day or two. When I explained my reason for killing him, he didn't say much anyway, there were hordes more of them.

We had scores of little sparrows that kept trying to build their nests just over the beams that were under the porch roof. It was interesting to watch them working so hard bringing one twig at a time to wind around another twig trying to construct a nest, but we didn't want them to build there because of the messy spots they left on the floor so we were constantly batting at them with the brooms trying to discourage them from building there. Then there were the crow families. Once they found a

245

good nesting place they just stayed there raising brood after brood, unless something very disturbing took place. It seemed we always planted our corn near their nesting place and they were forever feasting on this, their favorite food. Many seasons they would ruin a lot of the crop so our Dad held them in great disdain, but we had this little poem, bordering on superstition, that we always recited when we saw the crows in flight. It went like this: "one for sorrow, two for joy, three for wedding, four for a boy." Late in the afternoon or early in the morning Dad would get his double barreled shotgun, a few extra shells and hide out near the com fields. He knew how to imitate them pretty accurately cause the crows would invariably answer back with their "caw, caws." pretty soon they'd come flying over and Dad would unload both barrels on them. He'd had a lot of practice shooting crows so he always bagged at least one which he displayed in a very conspicuous place as an example for the others to see - hoping they'd stay away. The neighbors all followed the same procedure and between them all they kept the crows at bay.

Of course there were a lot of other kinds of birds, but I didn't come into close contact with them except in target practicing when my parents were gone. We mostly left them to do their own things, like catching insects and worms and messing up our money crops.

The Art Of Whittling

Usually in the winter months when it was warm enough to be outside, everyone tried to find something he could do on the outside so he could kind of "air out" in the warm sunshine.

As the local men gathered at the local store they'd begin sitting on the long bench along the wall on the outside till it was completely occupied, then they'd drag up a nail keg or two, or an old wooden crate, and one of them would brandish his pocket knife while he reached over and picked up a little stick and started whittling away. As the others had nothing else to do they would scrounge around and find little chunks of wood and join him.

Every farmer carried a pocketknife along with his "Brown's Mule" chewing tobacco in his overall pocket, so it was only natural for him to join his neighbors as they whittled away. Most of the time they were making nothing, but occasionally they would come up with a recognizable object.

It wasn't that the men could find nothing to do, they were resting, and that whittling required no concentration and very little effort. In fact, the lazier you were the easier you learned to whittle.

You didn't do anything without a "chaw" of tobacco, so they all bit off a sizable hunk of that habit and started slicing away. On some days the syncopated spitting and whittling went on for untold hours. The only other movements at this time were the adjustments of sitting positions on that hard bench and the kegs.

Mostly the conversations were about the crops and livestock or chickens, but every now and then someone would come up with a little bit of news, at which time the whittling stopped and everyone's head and eyes turned toward the news bearer. It was just like someone had said, "Freeze." After a few minutes of absorption and deep concentration, a conversation would emerge.

247

There'd always be at least one ole feller who couldn't hear so good so he'd blurt out, "What'd he say?" while the one nearest to him would attempt to repeat the news. He didn't get it out of his mouth before everyone else started correcting him and telling their own version of the tale. Before the day was over there were several different renditions going around and nobody knew for sure which one was right (pure gossip in its undiluted form).

It took a long time for the whittlers to wear that story out but after a while they got back to telling about how to cure up a corn or wart or "rhumatiz" or the best way to get shed of a cold. A lot of those cures and remedies were one for the birds, but no doubt those ole coots had tried them out at one time or another with fairly good results.

Pretty soon one of the more simple minded fellers would come ambling up smiling all over himself with his skippy teeth sticking out, a sordid, well worn hat on, and a flower in his overall bib. Everyone took time to acknowledge his arrival and ask him a few questions. He had a speech impediment, but he was always willing to engage in a conversation. After awhile he'd find something to sit on and get his knife out to join the others in their whittling. Someone would have to help him get his knife turned in the right direction so he wouldn't cut himself.

When one of the men's dogs came running up and sat down at his feet, that would trigger all sorts of wild tales about how smart his dog was. To hear them tell it, each man's dog was a prize winner and one of a kind, when, in reality, if they all came up at once you couldn't tell one from the other, and those rare qualities they supposedly possessed could only be seen at home by their owners. A few of them may have been exceptional in one way or another, but the other men were not gonna accept the fact that another man's dog was smarter than his.

One thing was for sure, the kids didn't get much bragging on back then don't know why the men thought it was against the law to mention their children out in public. Even that had some merit cause you didn't have to listen to the other men's exaggerations about their own kids. When everyone's rear end was numb, they'd stand up, stretch their legs, spit out their tobacco, and either get a fresh chew, smoke a cigarette or go inside and buy a "co-cola." There were all kinds of big glass containers of candy setting around for temptation, so one or two ole gents would pick up a piece and stick it in his mouth, while others looking around would remember his wife telling him to get a box of black pepper or baking powder, which he'd purchase right then and take it out to his chosen seat, all set and ready to commence where they left off with their whittling.

Some of them had finished their masterpieces of nothing and had to find a new stick to start on. One old man had worked for days on an original design for his own cane. He'd cut a while, hold the long stick up and take sight, then he'd inspect each side and hold the handle as if in use to see where he needed to do a little more work, then he'd switch blades on his knife for the real fine points. Everyone else stopped his own work to help him inspect his cane. Some of them were complimentary; others had all kinds of advice on how he could either make it look better or more comfortable to use.

The best articles many of them made were flip staff or handle for a hammer, or an oblong block to hold the pie safe doors closed, or a larger button to nail by the barn door to fasten it with. A toothpick for some would have been a good choice cause it could be finished in a hurry and didn't require much talent.

A few fellers with some ingenuity would carve a little rustic looking toy for his kid to play with or a new ball bat or a new churn dasher. Mostly, nothing was in mind when the whittling sessions started; it just provided a little enjoyment for the tired old farmers, who wanted to meet and chat with their friends, and if they happened to make a recognizable object that was a bonus.

249

Star Gazing

When the sun went down and the weather was "fittin'" after supper when all them dishes had been washed and some of us had taken our "spit baths," we'd congregate on our front porch till it was bedtime. Dad took his usual place near the end of the porch so he could spit his tobacco juice over on the ground and the rest of us filled up the swings and settees and chairs, while the smaller kids lined up on the steps. There were several wide steps that led up to the porch and they made good seats for those late-comers to the after-supper gatherings.

The first little while we mostly enjoyed the quiet as we watched the sun go down and marveled at the beautiful colors on the few clouds changing from bright to dark hues as the sun vanished. When the first star, or evening star, put in its appearance we all started making wishes and reciting the renowned little poem, "Starlight, star bright, the first star I see tonight; I wish I may, I wish I might have this wish I wish tonight!" Then, after all our refrains of that poem, other stars had begun to appear. Back then the skies were clearer and the stars brighter. On a clear night many constellations were very visible. The "Milky Way" was always fascinating and very prominent. We could spot the "Seven Sisters" easily when we were only three or four years old. The fact that there were seven of us sisters made that group special for us.

If anyone mentioned the "Big Dipper" or "Little Dipper" or the "Great Bear," we immediately found at least four sets of those and any and all other known constellations that we knew anything about, including the "Southern Cross." We weren't aware that it wasn't visible from our area; we just found a reasonable facsimile and were quite happy with our find.

It seemed like the heavens were all aglow with a million or more beautifully bright stars. In a way we enjoyed the evenings more when the moon didn't come out so early. The stars were much more entertaining for a while, but

250

like all other good things, we wore out the search and appreciation for them, so one of us would feel our way inside the house and find a guitar to tune up and chord around on, while almost everyone else joined in singing.

A few of us could harmonize, but there were no really accomplished singers in the bunch, we just sang for the lack of anything else to do. It was pitch black inside and the few kerosene lamps gave out such small amounts of light we weren't too interested in going inside.

Our Dad and Mom liked for us to play and sing together. Those were relaxing times and we enjoyed them till we ran out of words to sing, then we'd get the giggles as we made up our own words as we went along. After a brief time of giggling we'd start trying to scare each other. That didn't take a whole lot of thought. All we had to do was mention "mad dog" and every last one of us jumped up off those steps scrambling all over each other to get back up on the porch or even inside the door.

The first one inside the house would invariably jump out and yell, "Boo!" at the next one. Since we couldn't see in there, it would always scare us out of our skin. We'd get so noisy and rowdy our Dad would call a halt to our game and recommend (harshly) that it was time to get ready to "hit the sack."

As our Dad called it, "the first dark" had already gone and it was nearing bedtime. We usually went to bed and got up "with the chickens" as we had to get up early every morning to start tending to our various farm chores.

Some of us tried to sneak off to bed without washing up, but Mom, who was always thinking about those dirty sheets, would go down the line asking everyone if their feet were clean. There would always be two or three of us who had to march down the hall, pick up a pan and go to the kitchen to get some warm water from the kettle, find our wash rag, hanging on a line on the back porch, and then wash our outer extremities before we could go to bed.

In some of the bedrooms we could still see the stars from our windows. There was no need for shades or blinds, since it was at least a half mile and a few zillion trees between us and our closest neighbors. So we lay there and counted and admired those stars, trying to figure out what held them up there, till we finally went to sleep sometimes exchanging that magnificent view for a bad scary dream.

Exciting Cake Walks

A space walk had not come about when I was a child, but we did have cake walks. When the church funds for paying the preacher were exhausted, someone would come up with the idea of a cake walk. This was welcome news to most people, as "Mrs. Blabber-trap" got on the ole gossip machine and started spreading the news. It wasn't long till everyone near and far knew about the event. No one bothered to ask about the place. Everyone knew they were always held in the same place the community school house.

The next important thing on the agenda was making sure there'd be a variety of cakes. Since chocolate was almost everyone's favorite it was necessary to drop a hint to "Miss Know-it-all" that her delicious pineapple cake was a must for her to bring, since it had become synonymous with her name when cakes were mentioned. Several other kinds of cakes were kind of assigned to certain people to ensure the cherished variety. Every cook in the neighborhood tried to out-do her competition. If the cake ingredients were plain, she'd fancy the outside up with colored candy or nuts. It was terribly embarrassing to have your cake held up to be walked off and the ring not to fill up immediately.

When the final countdown for the cake baking came, our Mom would get everything together for her special choice of a cake and send us kids out of the house to play so she would not have little fingers coming from every direction pinching and sampling everything she had assembled for her masterpiece.

We were reluctant to leave at first, but when someone whispered we could slide on the "red bank" we all took off chasing each other, trying to be the first one there. The "red bank" was a steep bank of red dirt on the side of an old roadbed. The dirt, or clay, which was what the bank consisted of, was a good, smoothed down place to slide. If it was dry, the dirt dusted off easily but if it was damp the red mud dyed our underwear and was almost impossible to get clean when washed and scrubbed and boiled.

When we played sliding on our behinds down this bank we really tried to enjoy it cause we knew we'd most likely get spanked when we got home, for getting our clothes so dirty. After sliding down that bank a while we'd start squabbling about whose turn it was to slide next, which took the joy out of that game so we had to think up something else to do to keep us out of the house till our Mom's cake was finished.

If there were leaves on the ole sweet gum or poplar trees, we'd gather some of the largest ones, pick a few dried straws, sit down and break the straws up into short pins and fasten the leaves together into the desired lengths for belts, head bands, bracelets or ankle bands. We enjoyed getting all dressed up in those creations cause they didn't carry any repercussions. No one ever fussed at us about playing that game.

When we finally went back home and saw the yummy looking cake, we couldn't wait for the cake walk that night. These occasions brought out the whole community.

Whoever was in charge of the music came early to situate the ole phonograph, put in a new needle and assemble whatever records he could find that weren't scratched to a fare-you-well; some of the old favorites being "Birmingham Jail" and "Johnson Had an Old Gray Mule." Someone else was in charge of drawing the circles with numbers, as some others grouped tables on which the cakes would be displayed, while someone else made paper numbers to match those around the circle.

These numbers were drawn from a clear bowl when the music stopped, and were announced to alert the winner of that particular cake. Pretty soon everything was in order and the crowd started coming in. All of the kids gathered around the table of cakes to such an extent that an adult overseer had to stand guard to keep little fingers from testing icings or picking off nuts and candy.

The same person was usually in charge of M.C.'ing the affair and getting everything underway, as he made the loud announcement with his hands cupped on each side of his mouth that we were walking off a coconut cake, which someone else held up as high as he could, blurting out who baked it.

Most people had a favorite and waited for that certain cake to come up before they'd buy a space in the circle. When some cakes were brought up there'd almost be a stampede of folks wanting a place, while other cakes would hardly fill up the ring.

In the midst of the hoopla with all of its anxiety, there was a total concentration centered on the appearance of a tall, lanky ole gentleman as he entered, bringing one of the most sought after specialties of all "Mrs. Homebody's" incomparable caramel cake with little rows of pecan halves neatly lined all around the top. Mrs. Homebody herself never came, but she always sent that famous caramel cake, and needless to say, the circle filled up in a hurry when that cake was held up.

At this time the whole bunch of us little kids found our Dad and started hopping up and down and twisting our dress tails as we held out our hands for one of those cherished dimes so we could walk for that one. Our poor Dad scrambled around in all his pockets to come up with that much money, but he thought that cake would be well worth it. When the circle was filled, someone would start the music and everyone would move either slow or fast, depending on what number he wanted to stop on. When the music stopped everyone froze as he listened to hear what number had been drawn.

When that number was yelled out there was jubilation from the winner and his family and finger-snapping disgust from a lot of the losers, as they related how close they were to winning.

Not much time elapsed before the ring was filled up again, especially if the next best looking cake was displayed as the bonus. The whole process moved along rapidly for the first 12 or 15 cakes, but it took a lot of coaxing to fill up the ring for the last ones.

When all of the cakes had been disposed of, it was entertaining to watch the crowd disperse, carrying their loot home. It seemed all of the good luck ran in the same family as they carted off all the best looking cakes.

Sometimes we'd get home with a cake that didn't live up to its expectations. After a few slices it was hard to get "shed of". That was one of the reasons to get to the cake walk early so we could see who baked what. Oh well, since these cake walks were kind of charitable money raisers, we could always justify having blown a whole dollar in one night!

Good Ole Country Music

When you have very little else (materially, that is), a love for music with a small amount of talent can be a valuable asset in helping you maintain a decent outlook and your sanity.

Some of our friends and family were blessed with some musical ability, and we were all thankful for that. Obtaining musical instruments was another hardship, but somehow we managed to own an old upright piano, a guitar, and an old violin. My father played the "fiddle" in a real country way. His "Bile Them Cabbage Down" and "Soldier's Joy" left us kids thinking fiddling was squeaky and unpleasant sounding. He desperately wanted some of us kids to be good violin players. One of our sisters and one brother were the only ones to ever try to play, and that was strictly by ear, since there were no violin teachers nearby.

Almost all of us could "bang" a little on the piano, mostly by ear. Two or three of the older girls took lessons, but the rest of us picked up what we could on our own. The 'guitar chords were very easy and simple, so it didn't take anyone very long to learn them. Those "guitar players" were a dime a dozen all over the county.

The banjo players were fewer and farther between, as very few people bought banjos. Those players always drew a lot of attention wherever they were playing. The best I can remember, the special requirements for "tickling a banjo" were a few front teeth missing, or buck teeth, a big grin, thinning or bushy hair, and a thin lanky body. When you looked around at the spectators and spotted a few of the younger ones standing still with one foot on top of the other, pulling their gum back and forth, kinda keeping time with the plunking, you knew someone enjoyed that sound. I don't think the ole banjos ever needed tuning! The music always sounded the same till Eddy Peabody came along and played his banjo like a mandolin.

A lot of people owned inexpensive harmonicas, which we called "French harps." Most of these owners were too bashful to demonstrate their talent on these instruments. They required a lot of whuffing and snorting and shoving back and forth to create any harmony at all, so at best, that music was barely appreciated, but it furnished some enjoyment for the player.

Another unusual sight and sound was the "Jews' harp." They carried no melody at all and made a twangy, dull tone that came through with whatever accompaniment they had. Very few of our close associates even bothered to try to play one.

There were a few mandolins in our neighborhood, but there were very few players who could make acceptable music with them. When played correctly, these instruments made a delightful, jubilant sound as the player exerted a lot of energy strumming the strings real fast. At least they carried a melody that was recognizable.

One of the most popular instruments in our area was the old pump organ. Nearly everyone had one of these in their home. They were beautifully constructed and their lovely appearance made a lovely addition to anyone's living room. These organs had knobs that were located above the keyboard that had to be pushed in or pulled out to produce the proper sound. They also had two huge foot pedals that your feet had to pump constantly to help with the music making.

The seats were round swivel stools, and you had to play with a lot of gusto to achieve that loud roaring sound. Most of the tunes played on these organs were old hymns and you automatically expected a mournful sound when anyone rigged them up to play.

Dulcimers were few and far between. Don't know why they were not in more demand. I'm sure someone nearby could have learned to play one with a little practice and patience. All of the older gentlemen wore overalls, and the women all had aprons and sunbonnets, which seemed to be prerequisites for making that kind of music.

Horns of any kind were neither seen nor heard of in our area. We were acquainted with car horns; other than that we knew only about bugles which were used in the military and had only seen pictures of various horns being used in big city orchestras.

For those who wanted to play but had no instrument nor training, there was always the good ole comb and tissue paper, which sounded a lot like a kazoo. All you needed was a comb, with all its teeth, some tissue paper from an old shoe box and the ability to carry a tune. The procedure for this unusual music was to place the tissue paper between the comb and your lips and hum through your mouth. This could be played indoors or outside and never lasted very long, because of the ticklish sensation it made on your lips.

The playing of drums had not been introduced to our community. We thought they were only used by Indians to send messages on, and with all the noise we already had in our house, we were indeed fortunate to have been ignorant of this particular instrument's existence and use.

When Santa Finally Came

Nobody could convince us there was no Santa Claus, cause we heard him every Christmas Eve, and he always left us some goodies, and a lot of the times he left us what we wanted too. Of course, we knew what to want: nothing big nor expensive on account of there being so many others who also wanted something.

We had looked forward to Christmas all year long, ever since the last one, as that was the only time we were given gifts, except sometimes on our birthdays.

For some reason or other we never hung up stockings at Christmas, for one thing, we had to wear them the next day and our mantel was not nearly long enough to accommodate them all, and we always assumed Santa would only come down the chimney in our Mother's room. There were no beliefs that Santa would come down a different chimney, nor would he come in a door.

Since, we had always set a box for our Christmas presents, we continued the practice even though it took us a long time to find the right size box top or bottom to be used for that purpose. It took about as long to label the box and write Santa a message (including how good we'd been), in the bottom. The letter had to be real personal and different, sometimes we'd have to peep over at the others' messages to be sure ours were different.

We always went to bed early on Christmas Eve to make sure the fire went out and the chimney got cooled off before the man in the little red suit got there. We simply could not go to sleep early, but we pretended we did.

My Mother's room had about as many sleepers as a small motel. She was always crowded in the bed with two of the smallest children, while in the other double bed in the same room were at least two other kids. With a family of 12 children, at least two of the older brothers had already left home to live elsewhere; there were ten of us to be bedded down each night.

We had a room referred to as the boys' room, with two double beds, and another room which we labeled the girls' room, where all the older girls slept on two more double beds, and of course our Mother's room, which also had two double beds. As was common in our community, we also had a bed in our living room which was basically for company.

When Christmas Eve finally arrived, we placed our boxes all over our side of the foot of the bed to get a handful of candy or raisins and bringing it back to bed for us to gobble down before it was getting up time. Mom may have fallen asleep and didn't know what we were doing, but at any rate she didn't reprimand us, even though it was a dirty trick we had played on someone cause he didn't get as much candy in his box as the rest of us.

As soon as a little bit of dawn began to break through our Dad would bailout of bed in the boys' room, dress and start fires in the stove and the fireplaces. He was as excited as we were, but he wouldn't let us get out of bed till he had several fires going. By this time we were so excited trying to raise up and see what Santa had brought us we could hardly stand it. We were whispering and giggling and getting in position to be the first one out of bed when our Dad gave the ole "high sign." At that instant we'd jump and run around the boxes searching wildly for our own; of course, enroute we'd check out all the others to see what they'd gotten.

If we missed our box, our Mom would be fast to set us straight on which one was ours. She lay there on the bed and watched us for a long time. She looked 'so proud as she saw the happiness we were experiencing over our prized possessions! During all the confusion some of the older kids would sneak out the door and start shooting firecrackers, while the younger ones joined them lighting up their sparklers. That really made it seem like Christmas, especially when you'd hear several echoes from around the community of other kids shooting their fireworks.

When all the fireworks were gone we'd start really comparing our gifts and cracking those nuts that were in

261

our boxes, while we stuffed ourselves with raisins and candy. By the time breakfast was ready we were already filled to the brim, but we were forced to go to the table anyway.

Our Mom always fixed a super breakfast on Christmas morning and even sliced one of our favorite cakes, some of which she had stacked all over and in our two buffets or sideboards. She figured, along with our neighbors, that Christmas was 12 days long and had made preparations to that effect. A lot of our friends and neighbors visited and ate with us and we ate with them during these days, which gave us a chance to show off all our new gifts Santa had brought, while we ate up all that rich food that had taken our Moms so long to prepare.

When Anyone Died In "Our Neck Of The Woods"

It seemed like no one ever died in our community. Of course, the fact that I was very young made a year seem like a decade and most of the older folks really lived to be old.

Every family had at least one really old person living with them or in a house on the edge of their yard and they all seemed to be in extremely good health and were expected to live at least 500years. But and if one of them died there would be two or more to die within a short time. The only exceptions were if someone were killed accidentally (rarely) or a newborn baby died or in the case of the flu epidemic some people died because there were very few effective medicines known at that time.

On a rare occasion a sweet little girl died of pneumonia. This was a heart-breaker. Everyone assumed she'd get well, but with very few medications to use and poor housing and heating conditions the inevitable happened.

As the habits were when a local died, the men in the community gathered with picks and shovels and anything else that could move dirt and started digging. This hard and tiresome work continued till the grave was all the right proportions. In the meantime the womenfolk brought in all kinds of prepared foods while a few of the others made a pretty little shroud for the young corpse.

In those days some coffins were store bought, but many in our locale were home made because of the expense involved. The "good Samaritans" or neighbors were mighty generous when it came to helping out at a time like this, so they built a coffin and lined it appropriately for a decent burial.

Normally the dead lay in state at their respective homes. Most bodies were not embalmed so it was not advisable to keep them out over a day and night except if some close relative could not get there in that length of time. This involved a few more "corpse watchers" to sit up at night near the deceased.

These" sitters" were mostly men if a man had died and a few women if the corpse were a woman. I never knew why this old custom had to be adhered to and no one every explained it to my satisfaction. I still believe they were afraid the dead might come back to life and they didn't want to be alone with them if they did, or maybe they were afraid of ghosts that might come a-visiting in the witching hours.

When you walked into those dark, dimly lit rooms where the coffin had been placed with the lid up and saw the motionless, expressionless and quiet persons sitting around you could have very well wondered which one was dead.

If the death occurred in the wintertime there were no yard flowers to help cheer up the room so it was awfully depressing. In the summer those who had flowers brought a bouquet or made a makeshift spray and those were nice for a few minutes. They didn't compete with the "florist shows" of our modern day exhibits.

Those who came to "sit up" at the home of the dead made arrangements to stay all night if need be and "need be" meant if everyone else sneaked out around midnight and left almost no one there in the wee hours of the morning.

Those in attendance must have had a hard time staying awake since the very limited conversations were kept to a whisper. It was as the saying goes "as quiet as a mouse" in there, and there were occasions when mice were seen peeking around to see what was going on and why the lights were burning so late.

In cold weather a coffee pot with strong Luzianne was kept on a pot-bellied stove or on the hearth near the fire. This was a sure-fire "keeper awaker." At intervals the "sitters" would tip toe off to the kitchen where they'd taste of several of the foods that had been brought in and left sitting there. Just as soon as they'd left the "corpse room" they'd start talking louder or giggling if there were no family members listening. This helped to revive them temporarily.

When daylight finally came that last crew would go home to freshen up for the funeral. Many of them filled the choir seats to help sing those old sad, slow hymns for the funeral service. Several ministers were usually called in to conduct the service and I'm sure it was a real strain to come up with some flattering remarks about some of the un accomplished souls who never amounted to a hill o-beans while they were living their selfish, care-for-nothing lives. However, somehow they got through the service with those usual ordinary compliments paid the one who had passed and those usual condolences, the same, passed on to those of the family who had been left behind with the assurance that they'd meet them "over there."

All things considered, it was debatable whether the ones left behind were the lucky ones?

Restlessness Amid Poverty

After years of strenuous and tedious labor, with little or no compensation, the younger fellars, who would have normally been married with their own house at that age, were completely fed up with the status quo. Having learned through a letter from some distant relative about there being jobs in that state or city, they decided to set out under their own steam to seek their own fortunes.

Some left home carrying their earthly possessions in a neat little wad tied on the ends of a stick, which they hung over their shoulders. A few rode off on a horse or mule with their treasures and belongings in a box, while some others hitched up a wagon or buggy, packed up the family suitcase (a sturdy little oblong bag) with all their clothes and necessities and took off to parts unknown often only a few miles away.

Many of them wound up knocking on doors to see if the occupants could use any help on the farm or around the house. Their soiled clothes and untidy appearance often frightened the landowners, who would shut the door'in their faces. On a few occasions they would be lucky enough to be taken into the family unit to work as an extra hand for room and board, but mostly their pleas for work were rejected.

After days of walking and seeking, the hunger pains forced them to start asking for food. The only available food was leftovers or fruit from a nearby tree. There were no ready-to-eat snacks sitting around. A leftover baked potato was a real treat.

The local vagabonds would not steal, but a stranger often sneaked whatever he could see to eat. When these incidents turned out to be so commonplace, we referred to the "work seekers" as tramps or beggars, as few of them were earnestly trying to find work and better themselves, but most of them genuine "free loaders" and were mostly running from work.

Pretty soon, the larger town "over-runs" who were largely foreigners in this country, started coming into our area asking for handouts and helping themselves to whatever was exposed and loose. In this group were gypsies, who traveled in brightly decorated covered wagons, and they themselves wore gaudy clothes with gobs of shiny baubles.

They would arrive in full swing, dancing, singing and playing, creating a big fanfare to divert your attention from those who were roving around picking up small items which they hid under their skirts and jackets. When they left in great haste there was always a number of things missing, which they forgot to ask for and never did return. If fruit was in season, they'd stop by and gather a little on their way out from your place, and it wasn't unusual to hear a snitched chicken squawking as they rode away. Our parents almost panicked when they'd drive up, but us kids thought we were being highly entertained and hated to see them go.

As the days went by and things continually got worse, some of our more daring young and not-so-young men turned into hobos, trying to get to that far away place where Cousin Bob had this good job. Two or three of the fellars would get together and plot a plan to launch out, then they'd commence to gather their belongings and put them in a box and bargain with someone who had a running automobile to take them to the train station.

When they got there they would see scores of other such fortune seekers waiting around the depot trying to get in one of those empty box cars undetected. They stayed back out of sight till the ole engines started chuggin' real loud and fast, and then they "took off" running in a crouched over position to try to climb on board.

As the trains traveled along in the countryside. many of the hobos could be seen sitting on top of the box cars, but when they approached the next little town they'd scurry down to hide in the empty cars or jump off the train to hide on the outskirts of town.

267

There were numerous little campsites along the side of the train tracks where the "professional" hobos would cook and eat whatever they could scrape up for food. They seemed to be a congenial lot, as they shared whatever they had to eat with the less fortunate, even though it meant sharing a can of pork and beans with three or four others. If they were real lucky a rabbit or chicken would wander close enough for them to catch, dress and cook over the open fire for a real feast.

After they ate whatever they had, they'd sit around and play cards or make a little harmonica music to cheer them up, while some of the others sat around and whittled and told wild tales as they waited for the next train.

The switchmen, firemen, and even the conductors were mostly sympathetic with the hobos, as they favored them in any way they could, signaling when it was safe to load up or when the train would be leaving, even yelling out their destinations.

When these poor guys got to where they were going, they had a hard time finding cousin Bob, who didn't know they were coming in the first place, and when they did find him there was seldom a job waiting for them, or they looked so grimy and unkempt, cousin Bob wasn't too happy to see them. Many of them were forced to return home the same way they came and had to settle for a sharecropper's existence, living in an even more remote area with the barest minimum of household furnishings in an old rundown house.

Some of our older brothers experienced this kind of makeshift livelihood. Us kids thought a visit to see one of them in these old houses was the best of fun. We loved sitting on the floor to eat, sleeping on a pallet, and especially telling all the jokes we'd ever heard, playing checkers and jackstones (with real rocks) and making up and singing songs as the older brothers strummed the guitar.

Luckily, no one could hear us which was probably the best part of this whole scenario. These poor brothers and many others like them, made only enough from their crops to pay for the seeds and fertilizer and scanty food that had been bought on credit during the whole year.

Along Came Relief

Time had rocked along slowly till things got worse than "they could possibly be." Everyone was at their wit's end about a way to survive and pay their mounting debts at the local grocery and merchandise stores. Many businesses were going bankrupt and banks were folding. These were indeed troublesome times, resulting in many suicides.

As fate would have it, a presidential election year was approaching, and the candidate promising the most relief for the poverty stricken farmers and business world was naturally the forerunner. As soon as the elections were over we had a real progressive new president, whom the masses all but worshiped. He made long, personable, well-received speeches on the radio that seemed to address everyone's problems. At long last it looked like a new day was dawning.

The very best thing to happen in our area was the 3-C camps. Young men from almost every family signed up without hesitation. At these camps they received free medical attention (everyone's teeth needed attention), were given uniforms and furnished board in barracks located in many out of the way forested areas. Their jobs were building dams for lakes, making roads and bridges, and generally improving as well as beautifying our state and national parks.

Many of these fellars would have worked for the experience and board, but in addition, they were paid a salary! They'd never had it so good! And we were so proud to tell our neighbors where our brothers were (often no more than 100 miles from home) and what all they had seen?!?!

In addition to the CCC program, free food became available to the poverty stricken, which were labeled "commodities." Certain items could be obtained at specified community buildings, and by and large, they were a "God-send" for many families. Our father being the proud Irishman that he was would not permit us to get anything they had to offer. He called it welfare.

His general merchandise store was forced to close, as his friends, associates and kinfolks had carried off the biggest and best portion of his goods without any funds to pay for them or on them. His store ledgers were packed with unpaid entries, and he was too soft-hearted to take measures to collect for them.

As kids, we thought that was a delightful thing to happen, as we used our store for a playhouse. We dressed up in old lace-up shoes with spool heels, tried on the men's stiff shirt collars, found a few old hats and belts and really took advantage of a bad situation.

When planting time came in the spring, we went through the same rituals of planting the crops when a brand new program was implemented to aid the farmers. This required the farmers to plow up a certain portion of their cotton for a cash settlement. Who could resist that, with the threat of insects and inclement weather always a problem for the crops? Everyone jumped at the chance to receive ready cash! All of the older farmers scratched their heads in disbelief at such a thing! It was very sad for them to plow under those precious little plants that they had just weeks before struggled so hard to keep alive; however, who could turn down such an offer?

Many other new programs were approved and set in motion to help boost the economy, among which were the W.PA, N.RA, and the New Deal. With a little cash flow from several sources, many little businesses and manufacturers opened up shops, creating jobs for some of those choice people with a little bit of schooling and a willingness to work.

These jobs paid only a few cents an hour, but at least that was pay. One of my sisters worked for $1.50 a week and we thought that was big money. She even gave me a scorched and singed electricity-produced perm for a graduating present from high school. That was a "gift of all gifts" at that time and in our family. With all of her

271

other money she paid board and clothed and fed herself completely.

In keeping with all the other progress, there were even 8 to 10 cars a week running up and down the road by our house, and we were able to make some cash purchases at our local store. Once in a while we'd even buy a loaf of ready-baked bread to fix pineapple and banana sandwiches. We didn't have to worry about a spread, our mother always made her own "salad dressing," which is now referred to as mayonnaise.

Pretty soon our community was put on the map with a few electrical poles placed here and there. Words cannot express our jubilation at having those convenient drop cords dangling from the ceiling which gave us instant light!!

All of the kids in our family were growing up, and at long last, had something real to look forward to. Changes in every walk of life were taking place there as well as everywhere else, some for better, some for worse. But it appeared that the Lord had really heard our prayers and answered some of them, much to our approval.

BARE-FOOT TIME

Words and Music by
ELREE WORLEY

1. In the spring when it's wind-y and the show-ers come down, ___ It's
2. When the gar-den's all plant-ed and the bum-ble bees buz, ___ The
3. When the flow-ers are bloom-ing and the air ___ smells good, ___ The

cool on the out-side and it's wet all a-round, Then the days get
out-side's warm-er than it us-ta ___ wuz, Then the frogs start
birds are sing-ing like you think ___ they ___ should, And the young folks

long-er and the weath-er gets warm, and ___ the bees be-
croak-ing and the crick-ets chirp, must ___ be time to
thoughts ___ all ___ turn ___ to love, it will be time to

BARE-FOOT TIME

gin to swarm— I can play out - side, I can
go bare - foot — When my Pa - pa sits in his
go bare - foot— Oh, I got my wish and I'm

fly my kite, I can run and hop and skip and jump from
rock - ing chair, On the front porch in the shade where he can
jump - ing glad, Ma - ma said, "Ask Pa - pa," and my Pa - pa

morn 'til night; I'm so full of joy I just can't stay put—
get some air; I'll just walk right up with my pur - t'est look—
was - n't mad; He said I need not ask him an - y more—

Then ____ I won - der if it is - n't time to go BARE-FOOT.
When ____ he thinks it might be time that I can go BARE-FOOT.
Cause ____ the time had fin - 'ly come when I could go BARE-FOOT.

275

About the Author

Elree Bridges Worley was born January 25, 1924, in a very rural county located in upper middle Georgia. As a child her interests were drawing, painting, writing songs, skits and poems. This family was a close-knit one that was typical for that area and era. There were 12 living children, a very active mother, an aging father, and a paternal grandmother.

After many years of motherhood, housewifery and work in her husband's business, she started reminiscing about her childhood to her very young granddaughter who seemed very interested in the stories and wanted to hear more. With much consideration and thought, she felt it would be fun to surprise her sisters and brothers at their yearly family meetings with some little stories about their childhood antics.

In reviewing the fun times, it was inevitable to include some of the hardships and bad times. One story led to another and eventually she was encouraged to put them into a book.

Breinigsville, PA USA
16 February 2010

232589BV00002B/2/P